Fodor's 89
Montreal

Andrew Coe

D1149914

Fodor's Travel Publications, Inc.
New York and London

ISBN 0-679-01631-7

Fodor's Montreal

Editor: Kathleen McHugh
Researcher: Patricia Lowe
Art Director: Fabrizio La Rocca
Cartographer: David Lindroth
Illustrator: Karl Tanner
Cover Photograph: Guido Alberto Rossi/Image Bank

Design: Vignelli Associates

About the Author

Andrew Coe has written a literary column for the *San Francisco Examiner*, as well as articles for a wide variety of publications. He is now at work on *Fodor's Cancun, Cozumel and the Yucatan*.

Special Sales

Fodor's Travel Publications are available at special discounts for bulk purchases (100 copies or more) for sales promotions or premiums. Special editions, including personalized covers, excerpts of existing guides, and corporate imprints, can be created in large quantities for special needs. For more information, write to Special Marketing, Fodor's Travel Publications, 201 East 50th St., New York, NY 10022. Enquiries from the United Kingdom should be sent to Merchandise Division, Random House UK Ltd, 30-32 Bedford Square, London WC1B 3SG.

MANUFACTURED IN THE UNITED STATES OF AMERICA
10 9 8 7 6 5 4 3 2 1

Contents

Maps

Foreword

Montreal was discovered by a Frenchman, settled by French missionaries, and was, for nearly a century, a commercial and exploration center of New France. Today it is the third largest French-speaking city in the world, after Paris and Kinshasa, Zaire. And though the French culture predominates, the city is not thoroughly French. Waves of immigrants—Jewish, Chinese, Greek, Portuguese, Italian, Irish, Ukrainian, Vietnamese, among others—have, over the years, settled on this island in the St. Lawrence, each wave bringing its cultures and customs, and making the city multi-ethnic.

Montreal attracts more than 5 million visitors annually who come to explore Old Montreal, visit the many historical sites, shop in the Underground City, dine in fine restaurants of many ethnic persuasions, and be entertained at film, comedy, and fireworks festivals.

This is an exciting time for Fodor's, as it begins a three-year program to rewrite, reformat, and redesign all 140 of its guides. Here are just a few of the exciting new features:

★ Brand-new computer-generated maps locating all the top attractions, hotels, restaurants, and shops

★ A unique system of numbers and legends to help readers move effortlessly between text and maps

★ A new star rating system for hotels and restaurants

★ Stamped, self-addressed postcards, bound into every guide, give readers an opportunity to help evaluate hotels and restaurants

★ Complete page redesign for instant retrieval of information

★ FODOR'S CHOICE—Our favorite museums, beaches, cafés, romantic hideaways, festivals, and more

★ HIGHLIGHTS '89—An insider's look at the most important developments in tourism during the past year

★ TIME OUT—The best and most convenient lunch stops along the shopping and exploring routes

★ Exclusive background essays create a powerful portrait of each destination

★ A mini-journal for travelers to keep track of their own itineraries and addresses

We wish to express our gratitude to the Montreal Convention and Tourism Bureau in New York and Montreal for their assistance in preparation of this guide, especially Mary Baker and Willow Brown in New York, and Marilyne Benson and Gilles Gosselin in Montreal.

While every care has been taken to assure the accuracy of the information in this guide, the passage of time will always bring change, and consequently, the publisher cannot accept responsibility for errors that may occur.

All prices and opening times quoted here are based on information available to us at press time. Hours and admission fees may change, however, and the prudent traveler will avoid inconvenience by calling ahead.

Fodor's wants to hear about your travel experiences, both pleasant and unpleasant. When a hotel or restaurant fails to live up to its billing, let us know and we will investigate the complaint and revise our entries where the facts warrant it. Send your letters to the editors of Fodor's Travel Publications, 201 E. 50th Street, New York, NY 10022, or 30-32 Bedford Square, London WC1B 3SG, England.

Highlights '89 and Fodor's Choice

Highlights '89

One of Montreal's primary east-west thoroughfares and a central square were given new appellations—but not without controversy. Dorchester Boulevard was renamed **René Lévesque Boulevard** in honor of the popular Quebec premier who died in October 1987. (Street signs now show both names.) That done, there was a hue and cry that no site honored Lord Dorchester, the British governor-general who allowed French schools, churches, seminaries, and convents to continue in the new British territory following the Seven Years' War, essentially preserving the French language. Thus Dominion Square, in the heart of downtown, is now **Dorchester Square.**

It has taken 12 years to raise the money and construct the **retractable roof** over the Olympic Stadium, which was built for the track and field events of the 1976 Olympic games as an open stadium. The 26-ton roof that now makes it a year-round facility is made of Kevlar, the same material used in bullet-proof vests. It folds into a niche in the tilted tower by a series of winches and cables in a 45-minute process. Designed by French architect Roger Taillibert, the tilted tower is the tallest of its kind in the world. The observatory atop the tower—reached by 90-person exterior cable car—affords, on clear days, a 50-mile panorama of the city.

Montreal's era of mega-projects—thought to have ended with the Olympic Stadium and Place des Arts—is not over. Currently on the architect's drafting table are plans for what will be the **largest building in Canada.** The yet unnamed structure—a 78-story office, hotel, shopping, and concert hall affair—will be built on Boulevard René Lévesque next to the Sheraton Center. Don't start making hotel reservations yet. Completion is not expected until the mid-1990s.

Of more immediate interest is the unusual **Place de la Cathedrale** complex, scheduled to open in 1989. This startling project—an underground mall built beneath the Christ Church Cathedral—will feature 150 stores, primarily designer boutiques. The St. Catherine Street complex will also be connected to Eaton and La Baie via the Underground City. You may wonder whether the cathedral was moved during construction. No; the building was placed on enormous steel stilts while workers dug under and around it. At press time the cathedral had not moved one inch and services are still held there.

At the Montreal Botanical Gardens a **Japanese tea ceremony pavilion** opened in September 1988. The building features a Japanese garden, including many exquisite bonsai, and daily enactments of the Japanese tea brewing and drinking ritual. Visitors are encouraged to participate. The Botanical Garden grounds will soon be home to the **Montreal Insectarium.** Construction of the bug-shaped building began in late 1988, with a projected completion date of 1990. The building will house more than 50,000 insect specimens collected all over the world by Georges Brossard, Montreal's barnstorming entomologist.

La Ronde Amusement Park, the city's great summertime attraction, has added activities that focus on children and the elderly. The erstwhile Quebecois settlers' village has been redesigned into a children's village with exhibits, a petting zoo, etc. And a new viewing platform has been built for the ever-popular **International Fireworks Competition.**

Lachine Rapids Tours, which has been introducing people to the thrill of whitewater rafting since 1983, has added a third aluminum jetboat to its fleet. Peak summer-time capacity is now 500 rapids-runners a day.

Longer-range projects include a hotel-apartment complex on the site of the Old Queens Hotel at Peel and St. Anthony streets, a new hotel next to the Convention Center, and an office-apartments-shopping building in Old Montreal. All of these projects have a completion date sometime in the 1990s. One unanswered question for Montreal planners is what to do with Man and His World and the pavilions from Expo '67.

Fodor's Choice

No two people will agree on what makes a perfect vacation, but it's fun and helpful to know what others think. Here, then, is a very personal list of Fodor's Choices. We hope you'll have a chance to experience some of them yourself while visiting Montreal. For detailed information about each entry, refer to the appropriate chapters in this guidebook.

Special Moments

The 50-mile (80-kilometer) view from the belvedere atop Mount Royal on a sunny day

A leisurely *calèche* ride along the cobblestone streets of Old Montreal

Brunch in Eaton department store's ninth floor Art Deco eatery

The aerial pyrotechnics of the Fireworks Festival as viewed from St. Helen's Island

People watching at a sidewalk café on Prince Arthur Street on a warm summer night

A wet and wild jetboat ride on the Lachine Rapids

Taste Treats

A bologna, salami, and mustard-on-a-pretzel-roll sandwich with a strawberry soda at Moe Willensky's

Nibbling on smoked salmon, cheese, and pâtés at the Atwater Market

Poppy and sesame seed bagels—some say the best in the world —at Fairmount Bagels

A seven-course *menu de dégustation* at one of the top French restaurants

Off the Beaten Track

A film buff's visit to the Cinémathèque Quebecoise's movie museum and nightly screenings

The miniaturized furnishings of the Midget Palace

The new Insectarium, a temple to this bizarre and beautiful kingdom at Montreal's Botanical Gardens

St. Joseph's Oratory, one of the largest and most important Catholic pilgrimage sites in the world

After Hours

The elegant wood panel-and-leather surroundings of the Grand Prix bar at the Ritz-Carlton

Jazz riffs at the small, smoky L'Air du Temps

Avant-garde rock and wild styles at Foufounes Électriques

Thursday's, Montreal's liveliest singles bar

Rock, jazz, comedy—always a scene at Club Soda

Restaurants

Le Café du Paris (*Very Expensive*)

Les Mignardise (*Very Expensive*)

Milos (*Expensive*)

Cathay Restaurant (*Moderate*)

Les Filles du Roy (*Moderate*)

Hotels

Ritz-Carlton (*Very Expensive*)

Four Seasons (*Very Expensive*)

Hôtel de la Montagne (*Expensive*)

Château Versailles (*Moderate*)

Grand Hotel (*Moderate*)

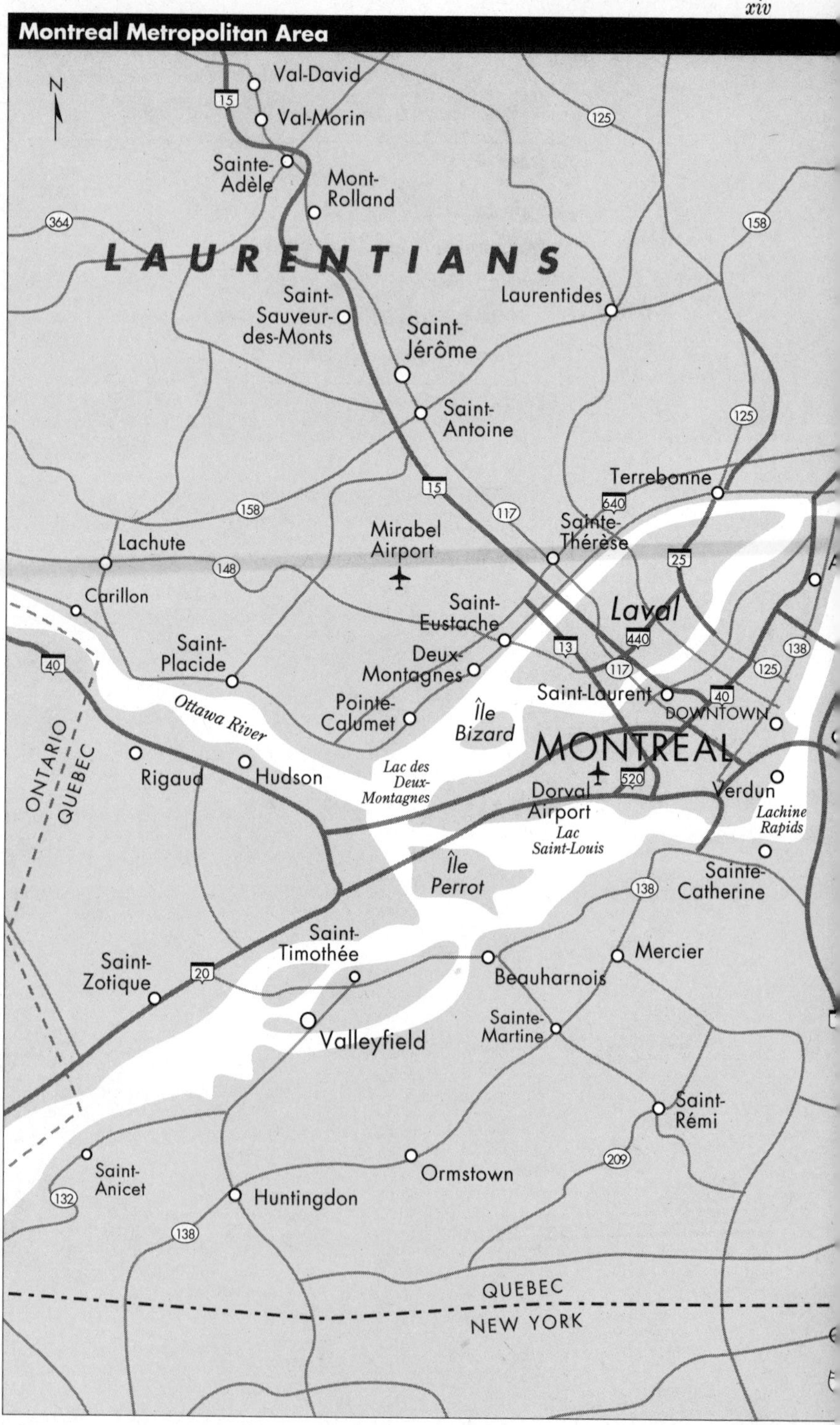

Montreal Metropolitan Area

N

15 Val-David

Val-Morin

Sainte-Adèle

Mont-Rolland

364

LAURENTIANS

Saint-Sauveur-des-Monts

Saint-Jérôme

Laurentides

125

Saint-Antoine

158

125

15

117

Terrebonne

640

Sainte-Thérèse

25

Lachute

148

Mirabel Airport

Laval

158

Carillon

Saint-Eustache

13

440

117

138

40

Saint-Placide

Deux-Montagnes

Saint-Laurent

DOWNTOWN

40

125

Ottawa River

Pointe-Calumet

Île Bizard

MONTREAL

ONTARIO
QUEBEC

Rigaud

Hudson

Lac des Deux-Montagnes

Dorval Airport

520

Verdun

Lachine Rapids

Lac Saint-Louis

Île Perrot

138

Sainte-Catherine

Saint-Timothée

Mercier

Saint-Zotique

20

Beauharnois

Sainte-Martine

Valleyfield

Saint-Rémi

Saint-Anicet

132

Ormstown

209

Huntingdon

138

QUEBEC

NEW YORK

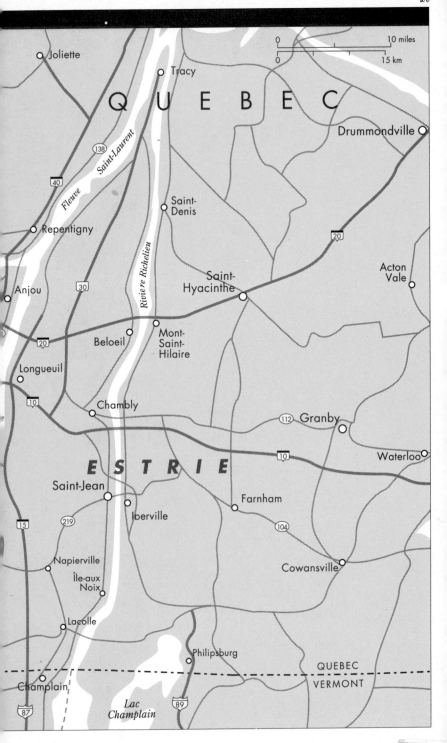

World Time Zones

MONDAY
SUNDAY

+12 +13   -9   -10

International Date Line

-11   -10

+11

+12

-4   -3

-3

-5   -4

-7   -5

-6   -4

-8   -7

-6

-5

-4   -3   -3

-3   -4   -3

25

+11   +12 -   -11   -10   -9   -8   -7   -6   -5   -4   -3   -2

Numbers below vertical bands relate each zone to Greenwich Mean Time (0 hrs.).
Local times frequently differ from these general indications,
as indicated by light-face numbers on map.

Auckland, **1**	Denver, **8**	New York City, **16**	Rio de Janeiro, **23**
Honolulu, **2**	Chicago, **9**	Washington, DC, **17**	Buenos Aires, **24**
Anchorage, **3**	Dallas, **10**	Miami, **18**	Reykjavik, **25**
Vancouver, **4**	New Orleans, **11**	Bogotá, **19**	Dublin, **26**
San Francisco, **5**	Mexico City, **12**	Lima, **20**	London (Greenwich), **27**
Los Angeles, **6**	Toronto, **13**	Santiago, **21**	Lisbon, **28**
Edmonton, **7**	Ottawa, **14**	Caracas, **22**	Algiers, **29**
	Montreal, **15**		Paris, **30**
			Zürich, **31**

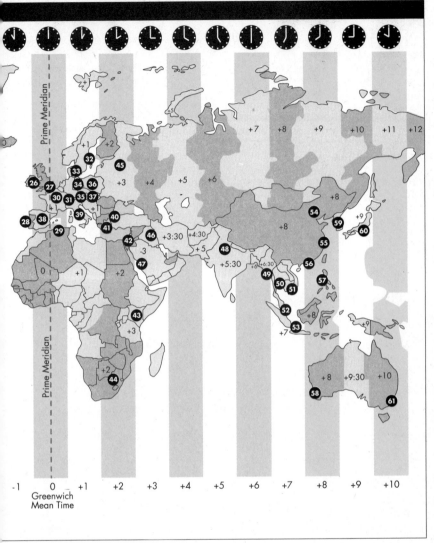

Stockholm, **32**
Copenhagen, **33**
Berlin, **34**
Vienna, **35**
Warsaw, **36**
Budapest, **37**
Madrid, **38**

Rome, **39**
Istanbul, **40**
Athens, **41**
Jerusalem, **42**
Nairobi, **43**
Johannesburg, **44**
Moscow, **45**
Baghdad, **46**

Mecca, **47**
Delhi, **48**
Rangoon, **49**
Bangkok, **50**
Saigon, **51**
Singapore, **52**
Djakarta, **53**
Beijing, **54**
Shanghai, **55**

Hong Kong, **56**
Manila, **57**
Perth, **58**
Seoul, **59**
Tokyo, **60**
Sydney, **61**

Introduction

by Patricia Lowe

A former reporter and editor for the defunct Montreal Star, *Patricia Lowe is a Montrealais who handles corporate affairs communications for the City of Montreal.*

Plus ça change, plus c'est la même chose," like other travel clichés, no longer applies to Montreal. For years, as Quebec's largest city and the world's third major French-speaking metropolis, Montreal clung to an international reputation attained in the heyday of former Mayor Jean Drapeau, who brought his beloved hometown the 1967 World's Fair (Expo '67), the Metro subway, its underground city, and the 1976 Summer Olympics. During his nearly three decades in power, Drapeau's entrepreneurial spirit added pizzazz to this transportation and financial capital at the gateway to the St. Lawrence Seaway.

But with the arrival of a nationalist provincial government in 1976, the mayor and Montreal were forced to rest on their laurels as the province agonized over its place in Canada. Separation from the rest of the country was seriously considered. The government passed Bill 101, a controversial language act (still in force), making French the official language of business and public communication. For the city it was a wrenching idealogical change; the only differences visitors saw were English or bilingual billboards and public signs replaced with French.

The ensuing unstable political climate produced sluggish investment and construction, which in turn affected the travel business. Tourist offices could only promote the standbys: the former Expo site (transformed into a permanent international exhibition center), fine French restaurants, and the historic attractions of Old Montreal—all worth seeing, but the city lacked novelty.

Montreal is again on the move. The provincial government elected in 1985 on a Federalist platform is creating a more upbeat environment. The more confident atmosphere has attracted corporate investment, transforming the downtown area with 12 new or soon-to-be completed complexes. Federal money is revamping the once-derelict old port into a vibrant harborfront, and has shored up smaller projects, such as Parks Canada's restoration of the gracious home of Quebec Father of Confederation, Sir George-Etienne Cartier.

The new roster of councillors has changed the face of the municipal government. It has been busy enacting laws to protect green spaces—like Montreal's most famous landmark, Mount Royal—adding more parks to congested downtown areas, and promoting development.

Without losing any of its French flavor, the city has added what some feel are much-needed '80s-style North American accessories. With its juxtaposition of old France and the new Quebec, Montreal is one of North America's more intriguing destinations.

The melding of old and new is no more apparent than in the flamboyant office tower of Les Cooperants. Even though the design of this 35-story pink glass structure imitates the Gothic-style Christ Church Cathedral it overshadows, it was not what the earnest French missionaries who founded Montreal envisioned. What today is a metropolis of 2.8 million—some 20% of other ethnic origin—began as 54 dedicated souls from France who landed on Montreal island in 1642. Led by career military man Paul de Chomedey, Sieur de Maisonneuve, they had come to this 32-mile-long island in the middle of the St. Lawrence to convert the Indians to Christianity.

They first set foot on a spot they called Ville Marie, now Place Royal in Old Montreal. Although they were pioneer settlers, Place Royal had been named by French explorer Samuel de Champlain, who established a temporary trading post here in 1611.

The first white man to see Montreal was Jacques Cartier, discoverer of the St. Lawrence, who stopped off on the island in 1535, interrupting his search for a shortcut to the Orient to claim this piece of the New World for France. Montreal owes its name to the navigator from St. Malo, although there are conflicting anecdotes on its origin. One has Cartier accompanying a welcoming committee of friendly Indians to their village, Hochelaga, supposedly on Mount Royal's southern slope at the site today marked by a cairn on McGill University campus. Scaling this mountain, and greeted with a splendid panorama of the river and hills beyond, he is said to have enthused "quel mont royal" (what a royal mount). (Visitors can enjoy this same view from the chalet lookout atop Mount Royal Park.) It is more likely he named it later, at the French king's request, in memory of Cardinal Medici of Montreale (Sicily), who had obtained papal favors for the King.

A truer tale has de Maisonneuve, more than a century later, in 1643, planting a cross somewhere on the same Mount Royal, in gratitude for the fledgling colony's escape from a flood that Christmas. The present 100-foot (30-meter) lighted cross—the glare from its 158 bulbs can be seen for 40 miles (64 kilometers)—at the mountain's summit has commemorated the first wooden symbol since 1924.

For nearly 200 years, city life was confined to a 95-acre (385,000-square meter) walled community, today's Old Montreal and a protected historic site. Ville Marie became a fur-trading center, the chief embarkation point for the "voyageurs" setting off on discovery and trapping expeditions (*see* Portrait of Montreal). This business quickly usurped religion as the settlement's *raison d'être*, along with its role as a major port at the confluence of the St. Lawrence and Ottawa rivers. However, the original Christian intent is still felt in the hundreds of church spires reflected in many a glass office tower and in street names like St. Denis, St. Gabriel, St. Pierre, and St. Sulpice.

Regardless of Montreal's enduring Roman Catholic nature, ever since the 18th century warehouses have been elbowing religious institutions for room. Entrepreneurs like John Jacob Astor, whose fortune was based on his early fur-trading ventures, put up sheds to store pelts; convents built stables and granaries, and later, grain silos rose up along the port. Former storehouses used for all kinds of commodities are today luxurious condominiums, shopping complexes, and offices like Les Cours Le Royer, off St. Lawrence Boulevard in Old Montreal, or the Youville Stables, now home to Gibby's, a popular steak house.

The old Montreal of the French regime lasted until 1759, when in one of the several battles of the Seven Years' War, British troops easily forced the poorly fortified and demoralized city to surrender. The Treaty of Paris ended the war in 1763 and Quebec became one of Britain's most valuable colonies. British and Scottish settlers poured in to take advantage of Montreal's geography and economic potential. When it was incorporated as a city in 1832, it was a leading colonial capital of business, finance, and transportation.

Montreal is still Canada's transport hub: It is home to the national railway and airline, the largest private rail company (Canadian Pacific), as well as the International Air Transport Association (IATA) and the United Nations' International Civil Aviation Organization (ICAO) at Sherbrooke Street's Aviation Square. But in the early 1980s, Toronto—already Canada's financial center—beat out Montreal as business center and most populous metropolitan area.

When Montreal was Canada's financial core, St. James Street was lined with the head offices of 15 banks and financial institutions. Most have moved, though some retain branch offices in imposing limestone and griffin-capped structures, reminders of their powerful past. Today the Bank of Montreal, Canada's first, maintains its headquarters in a handsome domed building facing Place d'Armes (a free museum off the lobby is open during banking hours).

Although financiers and lawyers preferred St. James Street, retailers moved uptown in the early and mid-19th century to follow their clientele who had begun to settle west, in the case of the English, east in the case of the French. These east-west distinctions are blurring but are still noticeable. In both directions, farming communities yielded to residential enclaves as Montrealers gradually moved out to places like Côte-à-Baron (now the trendy St. Denis quarter) or Notre Dame de Grâce to the west. The wealthy families of men who had made their mark in the brewing, fur, lumber, rail, and shipping industries—Molsons, Allans, Shaughnessies, and Van Hornes—had already built staid Victorian piles up Mount Royal, along Dorchester Boulevard, and, later, up and down Sherbrooke and its side streets, in an area which came to be known as "The Square Mile."

Solidly established by the late 19th-century, downtown today still reminds visitors of its grand old days, particularly along Sherbrooke Street, the lifeline of chic Montreal. The busy flower-lined stretch between Guy and University takes in the Mountain-Crescent-Bishop-Mackay sector, where sophisticated restaurants, cafés, and bars share canopied facades with haute couture salons, antiques shops, and art galleries.

This neighborhood earned its trendy reputation during Expo '67, the six-month international exposition that drew 50 million visitors from all over the world and marked Canada's Centennial. After touring the pavilions of 70 governments on the 1,000-acre site spread over Notre Dame and St. Helen's islands, vacationers would converge on Crescent Street's café *terrasses* and discos or Mountain Street's intimate little restaurants. Like the former fairgrounds and their popular amusement park, La Ronde, this stretch flourishes today as a major entertainment and cultural center.

Sherbrooke Street has preserved a number of its 19th- and early 20th-century lime- and gray-stone buildings—the castle towers of the Château Apartments, for example—and is the address of the Ritz-Carlton and Four Seasons (Quatre Saisons) hotels, as well as McGill University and the prize-winning architectural complex La Maison Alcan. International headquarters for Alcan Aluminium, the structure incorporates an old hotel and several Victorian homes into a modern office building. Free noontime concerts and art exhibitions are often staged in its lobby. The Montreal Museum of Fine Arts, emerging from its doldrums with shows featuring a master a year—Picasso in '85; Miró, '86; Leonardo da Vinci, '87; and Chagall, '88—and McGill University's McCord enthnological museum are also on this broad thoroughfare.

Peel Street, between Sherbrooke and Place du Canada, rolls through the Montreal most tourists visit. Its Dominion Square was renamed in a controversial and complicated changeover, a move that also saw Dorchester Boulevard on its south side rechristened René Lévesque Boulevard in memory of the late Quebec premier (from 1976 to 1985), just months after his death in October 1987.

Whatever the name, it has been the major tourist rallying point for more than 35 years. The recently renovated Dominion Square Building is the Art Deco home of municipal tourism offices and information bureaus. Bus tours, taxi guides, and horse-drawn carriages, *calèches*, all depart from some point around this public park. The square's monuments and buildings are insightful commentaries on Montreal's multicultural history. Statues commemorate such varied personalities as heroes of the Boer War, poet Robert Burns, and Sir Wilfrid Laurier, a Quebecker and Canada's Liberal prime minister from 1869 to 1911.

During the 1920s, the pillared Sun Life Building overlooking the square was the tallest "skyscraper" in the Commonwealth, and the classically elegant Windsor Hotel once hosted royalty. The Windsor now houses offices and an atrium shopping mall. Across the boulevard lies the "cheese grater" tower of the Château Champlain Hotel and the Roman Catholic Mary Queen of the World Cathedral topped by a row of solemn saints representing city parishes. Just one block east is the cruciform structure of Montreal's first modern-day high rise and the anchor of the underground city, Place Ville Marie.

Some visitors never make it beyond this area, which is a shame, because although the shopping, sight-seeing, and dining don't

disappoint, attractions farther south and east reveal more unusual aspects of Montreal.

To the east, St. Denis and the surrounding Latin quarter attract Francophiles, while a more ethnic flavor characterizes
the Chinese, Greek, Jewish, Portuguese, and other districts
around Prince Arthur Street pedestrian mall, St. Lawrence
Boulevard, and Park Avenue.

A bohemian atmosphere pervades Prince Arthur Street,
blocked off to traffic between St. Lawrence and Carré St. Louis. What the mall's many restaurants sometimes lack in quality,
they make up for in ethnic diversity—Chinese, Greek, Italian,
Polish, Quebecôis, and Vietnamese—and price, especially at
establishments where you supply the liquor (BYOW). Some
12,000 Portuguese residents live in the area's St. Louis district
and their bright pastel houses and lush front gardens have con-
tributed to the neighborhood's renaissance.

The Prince Arthur promenade ends at the once-grand Carré
St. Louis. Although its ornate Victorian fountain is spouting
again, it is still a dusty public square surrounded by 19th-
century houses, some nicely restored. A stroll across the Carré
brings you to St. Denis Street.

Early in this century, St. Denis cut through a bourgeois
neighborhood of large, comfortable residences. After a
period of decline, it revived in the early 1970s, and then
boomed, due largely to the opening in 1979 of Université du
Québec's Montreal campus and the International Jazz Festival
launched in the summer of 1980. Rows of French and ethnic restaurants, charming bistros, even hangouts for chess masters,
cater to Franco-, Anglo-, and allophone academics, while stylish intellectuals prowl the Quebec designer boutiques, antiques shops, and art galleries.

Activity reaches its peak during the 10 days every July when
some 500,000 jazz buffs descend upon the city to hear the likes
of Dizzy Gillespie, Montreal-born Oscar Peterson, and James
Brown. Theaters hosting the 1,000 or so performers range from
sidewalk stages to Place des Arts, the main performing arts
center in downtown Montreal, and Théâtre St-Denis.

The popularity of the jazz festival is rivaled only by August's
World Film Festival, also featured near this area at Place des
Arts and St. Catherine Street's Cinéma Le Parisien.

Place des Arts and the adjacent Complexe Desjardins constitute another intriguing hive of activity. Soon to be joined by
the Museum of Contemporary Art, Place des Arts is really
three separate halls built around a sweeping plaza overlooking
St. Catherine Street.

The main concert hall, Salle Wilfrid Pelletier, is home to the
Montreal Symphony Orchestra, which first came to promi-
nence in the 1960s under a youthful Zubin Mehta. It has won
acclaim for its "French" sound and classical recordings with
present conductor, Charles Dutoit. Les Grands Ballets
Canadiens also performs here as does the Opera de Montreal,
traveling companies of Broadway musicals, chamber orchestras, and guest artists. Place des Arts is linked to the "city

below" via its Metro station, and via tunnels to Complexe Desjardins, aswirl with noontime shoppers and hordes of picnickers relaxing by its fountains and exotic greenery. When touring around, remember city districts are spread out and, although parts of Montreal are within an easy stroll of one another, it is often a hike from east to west. The Metro, or subway, is an efficient means of whizzing from point A to B between 5:30 AM and 12:30 or 1 AM (have $1 in exact change ready, or buy six tickets, also good on buses, for $5.50).

One often-overlooked sector of the city requires a Metro ride but is worth the fare for a varied tour of Olympic and de Maisonneuve parks, the Château Dufresne Decorative Arts Museum, and the Botanical Gardens.

This triangle in the east end is distinguished by the flying saucer design of the Olympic Stadium completed by the world's "tallest inclined tower." An elevator speeds sightseers to its observation deck for a spectacular view of Montreal Island. A decade in the building, the tower is finally in place, 12 years after the Olympics it was supposed to crown. The highly touted retractable roof to protect the world's finest athletes was first tested as late as the spring of 1988. There may be critics of French architect Roger Taillibert's stunning tower, but it has turned into a big draw. If visitors time it right, they may even be able to fit in an Expos baseball game in the "Big O" (for its doughnut shape), their home turf.

Most Montrealers were convinced that the stadium tower, like the city's revival, would never happen. But as it inched up over the years, so did Montreal's mood, at times recapturing the spirit felt during Expo '67. In its present mood, the city should be ready to celebrate its 350th anniversary in 1992 with pride in its past and in its outlook for the 21st century.

1 Planning Your Trip

Before You Go

Government Tourist Offices

Contact the **Greater Montreal Convention and Tourism Bureau** (174 Notre Dame St. East, Montreal, Quebec Province H2Y 1C2, tel. 514/871–1595 or 871–1129) or **Tourism Quebec** (800 Place Victoria, Bureau 260, BP125 Montreal, Quebec Province H4Z 1C3, tel. 800/443–7000 in the continental United States).

Another excellent source of free information on Montreal and all aspects of travel in Canada is the **Canadian Consulate General** offices. Ask for the tourism department.

United States 1 CNN Ctr., Suite 400, South Tower, Atlanta, GA 30303, tel. 404/577–6815; 3 Copley Pl., Suite 400, Boston, MA 02116, tel. 617/536–1730; 310 S. Michigan Ave., 12th floor, Chicago, IL 60604, tel. 312/427–1666; St. Paul Tower, 17th floor, 750 N. St. Paul St., Dallas, TX 75201, tel. 214/922–9815; 300 S. Grand Ave., Suite 1000, Los Angeles, CA 90071, tel. 213/687–7432; 701 Fourth Ave. S, Minneapolis, MN 55415, tel. 612/333–4641; Exxon Bldg., 16th floor, 1251 Ave. of the Americas, New York, NY 10020, tel. 212/586–4200; 1 Maritime Plaza, Suite 1160, Alcoa Building, San Francisco, CA 94111, tel. 415/981–8515; 1211 Connecticut Ave., Suite 300, Washington, DC 20036, tel. 202/223–9710.

Tour Groups

When considering a tour, be sure to find out: exactly what expenses are included (particularly tips, taxes, side trips, additional meals, and entertainment); ratings and the facilities of all hotels on the itinerary; cancellation policies for both you and for the tour operator; and the cost of a single supplement should you be traveling alone. Most tour operators request that bookings be made through a travel agent—in most cases there is no additional charge.

General-Interest Tours "Eastern Highlights" from **American Express Vacations** (Box 5014, Atlanta, GA 30302, tel. 800/241–1700; 800/282–0800 in GA) visits Montreal, Toronto, Quebec City, Boston, New York, and Washington, DC.

Four Winds Travel (175 Fifth Ave., New York, NY 10010, tel. 212/777–0260) tours Montreal, Toronto, Ottawa, and Quebec City.

Maupintour (1515 St. Andrews Dr., Lawrence, KS 66046, tel. 913/843–1211 or 800/255–4266) offers an eight-day Montreal–Toronto tour.

Talmadge Tours (1223 Walnut St., Philadelphia, PA 19107, tel. 215/923–7100) has an escorted Montreal city package.

Package Deals for Independent Travelers

Air Canada (tel. 800/4–CANADA) has a two-night package with a choice of hotels—the cost depends on the hotel rating. **American Express** includes a half-day sightseeing tour in its city package. Also check the packages of American Airlines's **Fly AAway Vacations** (tel. 800/433–7300 or 817/355–1234) and **United Airlines** (tel. 800/328–6877 or 312/952–4000).

When to Go

Montreal is a year-round tourist destination. There is never an off-season, although between Christmas and New Year's Day it may seem as if half the city has headed for warmer climates. Autumn often arrives in mid-September, and the weather can be cold and rainy until the freezing temperatures set in in early December. Winter is long, cold, and snowy, but Montrealers—with their passion for hockey and skiing—revel in it. Those with thin blood take to the well-heated Metro system and the extensive network of tunnels and malls throughout Montreal that constitute the Underground City. Cultural life centers around the Place des Arts—a complex of three theaters in the heart of downtown—and it doesn't slow down just because the mercury dips below zero. From late November to early May many hotels offer a 50% discount, known as the "Montreal –50" package, on rooms for weekend nights. Spring arrives late (end of April). Come summer (early June), the whole city moves out of doors, and public life is punctuated with a series of sporting events and festivals celebrating the arts. Visitors and locals alike crowd Prince Arthur Street and Place Jacques Cartier to watch the street performers and to frequent the many restaurants and bars. Montrealers are determined to enjoy the weather to the hilt, so the nightlife doesn't slow down until the wee hours of the morning. Peak season begins with a literal bang in late May. Many countries compete in the International Fireworks Competition on St. Helen's Island that can be seen from points all over the city. Then there are music and theater festivals, major museum exhibitions, a Grand Prix auto race, jazz and comedy festivals, the Montreal World Film festival, golf and tennis competitions, and many more events through the first cool days in September. Although August and December get the most rain, they're not appreciably wetter than the other months. The temperature range is a little extreme: In July temperatures can crest at over 90 F, while during the depths of winter—from late December to March—you may encounter –15 F and below.

The following are the average daily maximum and minimum temperatures for Montreal.

Jan.	23F	– 5C	May	65F	18C	Sept.	68F	20C
	9	–13		48	9		53	12
Feb.	25F	– 4C	June	74F	23C	Oct.	57F	14C
	12	–11		58	14		43	6
Mar.	36F	2C	July	79F	26C	Nov.	42F	6C
	23	– 5		63	17		32	0
Apr.	52F	11C	Aug.	76F	24C	Dec.	27F	– 3C
	36	2		61	16		16	– 9

Current weather information on 235 cities around the world—180 of them in the United States—is only a phone call away. To obtain the Weather Trak telephone number for your area, call 800/247–3282. The local number plays a taped message that tells you to dial the three-digit access code for the destination you're interested in. The code is either the area code (in the

United States) or the first three letters of the foreign city. For a list of all access codes, send a stamped, self-addressed envelope to Cities, Box 7000, Dallas, TX 75209. For further information, phone 214/869–3035 or 800/247–3282.

Festivals and Seasonal Events

Montreal is festival city, especially from May to September, when celebrations of music, film, art, theater, and various sports abound. Major venues are the Place des Arts, St. Helen's Island, and the Old Port area. These festivals attract performers, entertainers, athletes, and visitors from around the world. Since many events coincide with the height of the tourist season, you are well-advised to make hotel reservations as early as possible. (Precise festival dates vary from year to year; for up-to-date information, contact the Quebec or City of Montreal tourist bureaus.)

Jan. 25–Feb. 5: La Fête des Neiges is a snow festival featuring ice sculptures and snowshoe, skating, and cross-country-skiing races. Notre Dame Island, Old Port, Old Montreal, Maisonneuve Park. Tel. 514/872–6093.

Mar.: International Festival of Young Cinema showcases the best in 16mm and video. Cinémathèque Quebecoise, tel. 514/252–3024.

May: SuperMotocross Laurentide features the national motocross championship as well as all-terrain vehicle, four-wheel van, and buggy races. Olympic Stadium, tel. 514/252–4679.

Late May: Montreal International Festival of Films and Videos by Women takes place at the Cinémathèque Quebecoise and other theaters. Tel. 514/845–0243.

May 22–June 4: Theatre Festival of the Americas is a showcase of new plays and productions from all over the Western Hemisphere performed at various theaters around the city. Tel. 514/842–0704.

Late May–June: Montreal International Music Competitions is a prestigious event featuring top young musicians from around the world. Place des Arts, tel. 514/285–4380.

Late May–June: Benson & Hedges International Fireworks Competition pits pyrotechnicians from Canada, the United States, and Europe against each other in dazzling displays on consecutive Saturday evenings in the skies over La Ronde Amusement Park. Tel. 514/872–6222.

Early June: La Classique Cycliste de Montreal is a professional cycling competition through Lafontaine, Mount Royal, and Olympic parks. Tel. 514/251–6946.

June: International Children's Theatre Festival of Quebec takes place at Lafontaine and other parks. Tel. 514/521–9084.

June: Le Tour de L'Île de Montreal is when 30,000 amateur cyclists circumnavigate the island of Montreal. Tel. 514/251–6955.

Mid-June: Molson Grand Prix is a competition of world circuit Formula 1 on Notre Dame Island. Tel. 514/392–0000.

Mid-June: Montreal International Rock Festival happens at the Spectrum and other arenas. Tel. 514/287–1847.

Late June: Lanaudiere Summer Festival is a mix of classical music and jazz that attracts 110,000 music lovers to this city 45 minutes from Montreal. Tel. 514/875–6986.

Late June–early July: Montreal International Jazz Festival is when 400,000 fans dig 1,000 musicians from 15 countries at sites scattered all over the city. Tel. 514/289–9472.

Mid-July: Drummondville World Folklore Festival takes place at this site 62 miles (100 kilometers) from Montreal. Tel. 800/567–1444.

Mid-July: Just For Laughs Festival is a multilingual, multinational celebration of comedy at various theaters. Tel. 514/845–3155.

Early Aug.: Le Grand Prix Cyclistes is a 124-mile (200-kilometer) cycling competition through the streets of Montreal.

Mid-Aug.: Haut-Richelieu Hot Air Balloon Festival and North American Championships takes place 25 miles (40 kilometers) from Montreal. Tel. 514/658–9675.

Late Aug.: Montreal World Film Festival is a prestigious event that draws top films and international stars. Sites: Cinéma Le Parisien, Complexe Desjardins, and Place des Arts. Tel. 514/933–9699.

Aug.-Nov.: 100 Days of Contemporary Art is an annual international invitational art festival. Tel. 514/288–0811.

Sept.: Montreal International Marathon attracts more than 12,000 competitors. Tel. 514/879–1027.

Sept.: Montreal International Music Festival features top classical performances at the Place des Arts and Palais dès Congrès. Tel. 514/866–2662.

Oct.: Montreal International Festival of New Cinema and Video takes place at the Cinémathèque Quebecoise and other theaters. Tel. 514/843–4725.

What to Pack

Clothing Fashion follows tourism in economic significance, and that emphasis is reflected in Montrealers' clothes, particularly when they head to night spots. Only in the fanciest restaurants is it necessary for men to wear a jacket and tie to dinner, and some of those waive that rule at lunch. The "DINK" (Double-Income-No-Kids) couples' hangouts downtown tend to attract a chic, pressed-jeans crowd. The cheaper dives around the universities draw the T-shirt and leather jacket student set. During the winter certain necessities overrule the dictates of fashion: a warm hat (preferably one that covers the ears), gloves, and waterproof boots. It is advisable to dress in layers: It traps heat better and allows you to shed a few "skins" when meandering through the Underground City. Furs are very popular outdoor wear, both for their warmth, as well as the city's historic reliance on the fur trade. (Animal rights activists haven't made much headway.) Many businessmen wear galoshes and must go through the awkward ritual of removing them when entering offices, hotels, and restaurants. No matter what the season, bring a bathing suit. Many hotels have indoor or well-heated outdoor pools that are open all year.

Miscellaneous Quebec operates on a U.S.-style 110-volt electrical system using flat, two-pronged plugs, so an adapter is not necessary.

Taking Money Abroad

Traveler's checks and major U.S. credit cards are accepted in Montreal. You'll need cash for some of the small restaurants and shops. Many establishments accept U.S. dollars. Although you pay more for Canadian dollars in the U.S., it's wise to buy some before you leave home to avoid long lines at airport currency exchange booths. If your local bank can't exchange your money into Canadian dollars, contact Deak International. To find the office nearest you, contact them at 630 Fifth Ave., New York, NY 10011, tel. 212/635–0515.

The most recognized traveler's checks are American Express, Barclay's, Thomas Cook, and those issued through major commercial banks such as Citibank and Bank of America. Some banks will issue the checks free to established customers, but most charge a 1% commission fee. Buy part of the traveler's checks in small denominations to cash toward the end of your trip. This will save you from having to cash a large check and ending up with more foreign money than you need. You can also buy traveler's checks in Canadian dollars, a good idea if the U.S. dollar is falling and you want to lock in the current rate. Remember to take the addresses of offices where you can get refunds for lost or stolen traveler's checks.

Banks and bank-operated currency-exchange kiosks in airports, railway stations, and bus terminals are the best places to change money. Hotels and privately run exchange firms will give you a significantly lower rate of exchange.

Like the American dollar, the Canadian one floats (and often sinks) on the world's money markets, but it will probably remain in the U.S. 70¢–75¢ range for the foreseeable future. As of 1987, the one-dollar bill is being phased out in Canada and replaced with a funny-looking coin that has already been nicknamed "The Loonie," due to the drawing of the Canadian loon on one side. But these bills (as well as the far more useful $5-, $10-, and $20- bills—and, yes, the always welcome $2 Canadian denomination) should remain in circulation into the 1990s.

U.S. currency is eagerly accepted at most good-size stores and restaurants, and with good reason. Owners are always happy to give far less exchange than the daily rate–even as little as 10¢ or 15¢ on the dollar. So it is financially wise for all visitors to go to a Canadian bank or exchange firm within a few hours of arrival. The sooner you exchange your money for the worth-less (if not yet worthless) Canadian dollar, the more money you'll save. When you use your credit cards, you can be assured that your expenditures will automatically go through as Canadian funds, and you will get the proper exchange rate.

Montreal banks have rather abbreviated hours—usually weekdays from 10 AM to 3 or 4 PM. Those with extended hours include: **Royal Bank of Canada,** Place Ville Marie (Mon., Tues., Wed., and Fri. 9–5, Thurs. 9:30–5:30, tel. 514/874–2110); **Canadian National Bank,** Complexe Desjardins (daily except Mon. and Tues. 9–5, tel. 514/281–9650); **Bank of Montreal,** Les Terrasses, next to Eaton department store (weekdays 8:30–5, Sat. 10–4, tel. 514/877–1710). The major currency exchange bureaus are **Bank of America** (800 René Lévesque Blvd. W, tel. 514/879–1200), **Deak International** (625 René Lévesque Blvd. W, tel. 514/397–0004), **Guardian** (18 St. Jacques St., tel. 514/842–7161), and **National Coin Exchange** (1240 Peel St., tel. 514/879–1300).

Getting Money from Home

There are at least three ways to get money from home: (1) Have it sent through a large commercial bank with a branch in Toronto. The only drawback is that you must have an account with the bank; if not, you'll have to go through your own bank and the process will be slower and more expensive. (2) Have it sent through American Express. If you are a cardholder, you can cash a personal check or a counter check at an American Express office for up to $1,000; $200 will be in cash and $800 in traveler's checks. There is a 1% commission on the traveler's checks. You can also receive money through American Express MoneyGram. With this service, you can receive up to $5,000 cash. It works this way: You call home and ask someone to go to an American Express office or an American Express MoneyGram agent located in a retail outlet, and fill out an American Express MoneyGram. It can be paid for with cash or any major credit card. The person making the payment is given a reference number and telephones you with that number. The American Express MoneyGram agent calls an 800 number and authorizes the transfer of funds to an American Express office or participating agency in Montreal. In most cases, the money is available immediately. You pick it up by showing identification and giving the reference number. Fees vary according to the amount of money sent. For sending $300, the fee is $22; for $5,000, $150. For the American Express MoneyGram location nearest your home, call 800/543–4080. You do not have to be a cardholder to use this service. (3) Have it sent through Western Union (tel. 800/325–6000). If you have MasterCard or Visa, you can have money sent for any amount up to your credit limit. If not, have someone take cash or a certified cashier's check to a Western Union office. The money will be delivered to a bank in Montreal within 24 hours. Fees vary with the amount of money sent. For sending $500, the fee is $35; for $1,000, $45.

Canadian Currency

At press time, the U.S. dollar is worth about 30% more than its Canadian counterpart. This makes traveling in Canada particularly advantageous for American citizens. Spending $50 (Canadian) for two on dinner comes out to about $35 (U.S.). And what you get for your money even at $50 almost always represents excellent value.

Currency can be changed at bank-operated kiosks at airports and rail and bus terminals on weekends as well as during business hours. Most hotels and restaurants will also convert money, but usually at rates below those offered by banks. Currency is based on the same decimal system as in the United States and with the same denominations. An added bonus is the $2 bill, which is alive and well in Canada.

Credit cards are accepted just about everywhere a tourist might visit. The best known are American Express, Visa, and

MasterCard. Major credit cards use the exchange rate in effect on the date of the transaction. For safety and convenience, carry traveler's checks. You can buy them in Canadian dollars at most commercial banks—a good idea if the U.S. dollar is falling and you want to lock in the current exchange rate.

What It Will Cost

American and British visitors to Montreal will find the city a bargain, as long as the current exchange rates hold up. Those packing a strong currency will find all the necessities moderately priced.

Sample Prices in U.S. $ (1988)

Cup of coffee or soda	$1
Glass of wine	$3.50
Croque-monsieur (ham-and-cheese sandwich)	$4
Hamburger	$2.50–$5

Taxes A 9% sales tax applies to all goods and services except hotel rooms, books, home furnishings, shoes costing less than $125, and clothes under $500. There is a 10% meal tax on all orders costing more than $3.25. At press time there is talk of reinstating the 10% sales tax on hotel rooms. A budget double room runs from $15 to $50, while a luxury suite can cost well above $200. Dinner at the most expensive restaurants can cost from $30 to $100 per person, but you can eat very well for less than $10. Taxi rates begin with a $2 minimum, with an increase of 70¢/kilometer thereafter. Bus and Metro fares are $1.

Passports and Visas

American Because there is so much border traffic between Canada and the United States—many people live in Windsor, Ontario, and work in Detroit, for example—entry requirements are fairly simple. Citizens and legal residents of the United States do not require a passport or a visa to enter Canada, though valid identification (passport or birth certificate) may be requested. Resident aliens should be in possession of their U.S. Alien Registration or green card.

British Citizens of the United Kingdom are also exempt from possessing a passport or visa, though proof of citizenship is required.

Customs and Duties

On Arrival Clothing, personal items, and any professional tools or equipment (if you work in Canada), can be brought in without charge or restriction. American and British visitors can bring in the following items duty-free: 200 cigarettes, 50 cigars, and 2 pounds of tobacco; personal cars (for less than six months); boats or canoes; rifles and shotguns (but no handguns or automatic weapons); 200 rounds of ammunition; cameras, radios, sports equipment, and typewriters. A deposit is sometimes required for trailers and household equipment (refunded upon return), and if you are driving a rental car, be sure and keep the contract with you. Cats may enter freely, but dogs must have proof of a veterinary inspection to ensure that they are free of communicable diseases, such as rabies. Plant material must be declared and inspected.

On Departure   Passengers flying from Montreal to the United States will clear U.S. Customs in Montreal, so allow extra time before your flight. If you have brought any foreign-made equipment from home, such as cameras, it's wise to carry the original receipt with you or register it with U.S. Customs before you leave (Form 4457). Otherwise you may end up paying duty on your return. **U.S. residents** visiting Canada for at least 48 hours may bring home up to $400 in foreign goods duty-free. Each member of the family is entitled to the same exemption, regardless of age, and exemptions can be pooled. For the next $1,000 worth of goods, a flat 10% rate is assessed; above $1,400, duties vary with the merchandise. Included for travelers 21 or older are one liter of alcohol, 100 cigars (non-Cuban), and 200 cigarettes. Only one bottle of perfume trademarked in the United States may be brought in. However, there is no duty on antiques or art more than 100 years old. Anything exceeding these limits will be taxed at the port of entry, and may be taxed additionally in the traveler's home state. Gifts valued at less than $50 may be mailed duty-free to friends or relatives at home, but not more than one package per day to any one addressee and not to include perfumes costing more than $5 or tobacco or liquor.

Tips for British Travelers

Government Tourist Offices   **Tourism Canada,** (Canada House, Trafalgar Sq., London SW1Y 5BJ, tel. 01/629–9492) will send you brochures and information on Montreal, and advise you on your trip.

Passports and Visas   You will need a valid passport (cost, £15). Visas and vaccinations are not required.

Customs   Returning to Britain you may bring home: (1) 200 cigarettes or 100 cigarillos or 50 cigars or 250 grams of tobacco; (2) two liters of table wine and, in addition, (a) one liter of alcohol over 22% by volume (most spirits), (b) two liters of alcohol under 22% by volume (fortified or sparkling wine), or (c) two more liters of table wine; (3) 50 grams of perfume and ¼ liter of toilet water; and (4) other goods up to a value of £32.

Insurance   To cover health and motoring mishaps, insure yourself with **Europ Assistance** (252 High St., Croydon, Surrey CR0 1NF, tel. 01/680–1234).

It is also wise to take out insurance to cover loss of luggage (though make sure this isn't already covered in your existing homeowner's policy). Trip cancellation insurance is another wise buy. The **Association of British Insurers** (Aldermary House, Queen St., London EC4N 1TT, tel. 01/248–4477) will give comprehensive advice on all aspects of vacation insurance.

Tour Operators   Many packages include car rentals at reasonable rates. **National Holidays Ltd.** (George House, George St., Wakefield, West Yorkshire WF1 1LY, tel. 0924/383–888) will put together a complete package to Canada, with flights, from £289, or a week's car rental alone, from £88. Similar schemes are offered by **Hickie Borman Holidays** (73 High St., Ewell, Surrey KT17 1RX, tel. 01/393–0127) and **American Airplan** (Box 267, Walton-on-Thames, Surrey KT12 2TS, tel. 0932/246–166).

Airfares   Round-trip APEX fares to Montreal cost about £315. Major airlines serving Montreal are **Air Canada,** tel. 01/759–2636;

British Airways, tel. 01/897–4000; **Northwest Airlines,** tel. 01/629–5353; and **Wardair,** tel. 0345/222333. Travel agents can book charter flights through Regent Tours; the carrier is Worldways. If you can afford to be flexible about when you travel, look for last-minute flight bargains advertised in the Sunday newspapers. Round-trip fares at press time cost about £160.

Traveling with Film

If your camera is new, shoot and develop a few rolls of film before leaving home. Pack some lens tissue, and don't forget an extra battery for your built-in light meter. Invest about $10 in a skylight filter and screw it onto the front of your lens. It will protect the lens and also reduce haze.

Film doesn't like hot weather. In summer, don't store film in a car glove compartment or on the shelf under the rear window; put it behind the front seat on the floor, away from the exhaust pipe.

On a plane trip, never pack unprocessed film in check-in luggage; if your bags get X-rayed, say good-bye to your pictures. Always carry undeveloped film with you through security checks and ask to have it inspected by hand. (It helps to isolate your film in a plastic bag, so it's ready for quick inspection.) Inspectors at U.S. airports are required by law to honor requests for hand inspection; abroad, you'll have to depend on the kindness of strangers.

The old airport scanning machines—still in use in some Third World countries—use heavy doses of radiation that can turn a family portrait into an early morning fog. The newer models—used in all U.S. airports—are safe for anything from five to 500 scans, depending on the speed of your film. The effects are cumulative; you can put the same roll of film through several scans without worry. After five scans, though, you're asking for trouble.

If your film gets fogged and you want an explanation, send it to the **National Association of Photographic Manufacturers.** (600 Mamaroneck Ave., Harrison, NY 10528). NAPM representatives will try to determine what went wrong. The service is free.

Language

French is the official language of the Province of Quebec, which includes Montreal. Many people also speak English, however, and, in certain neighborhoods like Westmount, only English is spoken. Downtown, the majority of the people are bilingual. Neighborhoods like St. Denis, Outremont, and Mount Royal are primarily French-speaking, and some shopkeepers here don't speak English. In the past tourists have encountered instances of Francophone snobbery in hotels and restaurants, but this happens ever more rarely. The Quebec government, realizing how much tourism means to the economy, has enacted laws stating that menus, hotel brochures, and other tourist literature must be printed in both languages. The tension between Quebec and the rest of Canada and between French and English speakers has lessened in recent years, thus making it easier for English-speaking tourists.

Staying Healthy

Shots and Medications There are no health risks associated with travel to Canada and inoculations are not needed. If you have a health problem that might require purchasing prescription drugs while in the country, have your doctor write a prescription using the drug's generic name. Brand names vary widely from country to country.

The **International Association for Medical Assistance to Travelers** (IAMAT) is a worldwide association offering a list of approved, English-speaking doctors whose training meets U.S. standards. For a list of Canadian physicians and clinics that are part of this network, contact IAMAT, 736 Center St., Lewiston, NY 14092. In Canada: 188 Nicklin Rd., Guelph, Ontario, N1H 7L5. In Europe: Gotthardstrasse 17, 6300 Zug, Switzerland. Membership is free.

Insurance

Travelers may seek insurance coverage in three areas: health and accident, loss of luggage, and trip cancellation. Your first step is to review your existing health and homeowner policies; some health insurance plans cover health expenses incurred while traveling, some major medical plans cover emergency transportation, and some home-owner policies cover the theft of luggage.

Health and Accident Several companies offer coverage designed to supplement existing health insurance for travelers:

Carefree Travel Insurance (Box 310, 120 Mineola Blvd., Mineola, NY 11501, tel. 800/645–2424 or 516/294–0220) provides coverage for medical evacuation. It also offers 24-hour medical advice by phone.

Health Care Abroad, International Underwriters Group (243 Church St. West, Vienna, VA 22180; tel. 800/237–6615 or 703/281–9500), offers comprehensive medical coverage, including emergency medical evacuation, for trips of 10 to 90 days.

International SOS Insurance (Box 11568, Philadelphia, PA 19116, tel. 800/523–8930 or 215/244–1500) does not provide medical insurance but arranges medical evacuations for its clients, who are often international corporations.

Travel Guard International, (1100 Centerpoint Dr., Stevens Point, WI 54481, tel. 800/782–5151 or 715/345–0505), underwritten by Cygna, offers medical insurance, with coverage for emergency evacuation when Travel Guard's representatives in the United States say it is necessary.

Loss of Luggage Luggage loss coverage is usually part of a comprehensive travel insurance package that includes personal accident, trip cancellation, and sometimes default and bankruptcy. Several companies offer broad policies:

Access America Inc., a subsidiary of Blue Cross-Blue Shield, Box 807, New York, NY 10163, tel. 800/851–2800.

Near, Inc., 1900 N. MacArthur Blvd., Suite 210, Oklahoma City, OK 73127, tel. 800/654–6700.

Travel Guard International *(see* Health and Accident Insurance).

Trip Cancellation Flight insurance is often included in the price of a ticket when purchased with American Express, Visa, or another major credit card. It is usually included in travel insurance packages available from many tour operators, travel agents, and insurance agents.

Renting Cars

If you're flying to Montreal and plan to spend some time there before exploring the rest of Quebec, save money by arranging to pick up your car in the city and then head off into the province. You'll have to weigh the added expense of renting a car from a major company with an airport location against the savings on a car from a budget firm with offices in town. You could waste precious hours trying to locate the budget company in return for only small financial savings. If you're arriving and departing from different airports, look for a one-way car rental with no drop-off charge. Rental rates vary widely, depending on the size and model, number of days you use the car, insurance coverage, and whether or not drop-off fees are imposed. In most cases, rates quoted include unlimited free mileage and standard liability protection. Not included are Collision Damage Waiver (CDW), which eliminates your deductible payment should you have an accident; personal accident insurance; gasoline; and 10% sales tax.

Drivers' licenses issued in the United States are valid in Canada. And though the driving age in Canada is 16, you must be 21 to rent a car. It's best to arrange a car rental before you leave home. You won't save money by waiting until you arrive in Montreal, and the type of car you prefer may not be available at the last minute. Rental companies usually charge according to the exchange rate of the U.S. dollar at the time the car is returned or when the credit card payment is processed. Rental car companies that serve Montreal include **Avis** (1225 Metcalfe St., Metro Peel, tel. 514/866–7906 or 800/268–0303), **Budget** (1460 Guy St., Metro Guy-Concordia, tel. 514/937–9121 or 800/268–8900); **Hertz** (1475 Aylmer St., Metro McGill, tel. 514/842–8537 or 800/263–0600); and **Tilden** (1200 Stanley St., Metro Peel, tel. 514/878–2771 or 800/361–5334).

Student and Youth Travel

The **International Student Identity Card (ISIC)** entitles students to youth rail passes, special fares on local transportation, and discounts at museums, theaters, sports events, and many other attractions. If purchased in the United States, the $10 cost of the ISIC also includes $2,000 in emergency medical insurance, plus $100 a day for up to 60 days of hospital coverage. Apply to the Council on International Student Exchange (CIEE 205 E. 42nd St., New York, NY 10017, tel. 212/661–1414). In Canada, the ISIC is available from the Federation of Students-Services (187 College St., Toronto, Ontario M5T 1P7) for CN$10.

Council Travel, a CIEE subsidiary, is the foremost U.S. student travel agency, specializing in low-cost charters and serving as the exclusive U.S. agent for many student airfare bargains and student tours. CIEE's 80-page *Student Travel Catalog* and "Council Charter" brochure are available free from any Council Travel office in the U.S. (enclose $1 postage if ordering by mail). In addition to the CIEE headquarters at 205 East 42nd Street and a branch office at 35 West 8th Street in New York City, there are Council Travel offices in Amherst, Austin, Berkeley, Boston, Cambridge, Chicago, Dallas, La Jolla, Long Beach, Los Angeles, Portland, Providence, San Diego, San Francisco, and Seattle.

The **Educational Travel Center** (438 N. Frances St., Madison, WI 55703, tel. 608/256–5551),another student travel specialist, is worth contacting for information on student tours, bargain fares, and booking.

Students who would like to work abroad should contact *CIEE's Work Abroad Department* (at 205 E. 42nd St., New York, NY 10017). The council arranges various types of paid and voluntary work experiences overseas for up to six months. CIEE also sponsors study programs in Latin America, Asia, and publishes many books of interest to the student traveler: These include *Work, Study, Travel Abroad: The Whole World Handbook* ($8.95 plus $1 postage); *Work Your Way Around the World* ($10.95 plus $1 postage); and *Volunteer! The Comprehensive Guide to Voluntary Service in the U.S. and Abroad* ($5.50 plus $1 postage).

The Information Center at the **Institute of International Education**, IIE (809 UN Plaza, New York, NY 10017, tel. 212/984–5413), has reference books, foreign university catalogues, study-abroad brochures, and other materials, which may be consulted by students and nonstudents alike, free of charge. The Information Center is open from 10 to 4, Mon.–Fri., and until 7 Wed.

IIE administers a variety of grant and study programs offered by U.S. and foreign organizations, and publishes a well-known annual series of study-abroad guides, including *Academic Year Abroad, Vacation Study Abroad,* and *Study in the United Kingdom and Ireland.* The institute also publishes *Teaching Abroad,* a book of employment and study opportunities overseas for U.S. teachers. For a current list of IIE publications, prices, and ordering information, write to Publications Service, Institute of International Education, 809 UN Plaza, New York, NY 10017. Books must be purchased by mail or in person; telephone orders are not accepted.

General information on IIE programs and services is available from its regional offices in Atlanta, Chicago, Denver, Houston, San Francisco, and Washington, DC

Traveling with Children

Publications *Family Travel Times,* an 8- or 12-page newsletter is published 10 times a year by TWYCH (Travel with Your Children, 80 Eighth Ave., New York, NY 10011, tel. 212/206–0688). Subscription includes access to back issues and twice-weekly opportunities to call in for specific information.

Villa Rentals **At Home Abroad, Inc.,** 405 E. 56th St., Suite 6H, New York, NY 10022, tel. 212/421–9165; **Villas International,** 71 W. 23rd St., New York, NY 10010, tel. 212/929–7585 or 800/221–2260; **Hideaways, Inc.,** Box 1464, Littleton, MA 01460, tel. 617/486–8955; **Villas and Apartments Abroad,** 444 Madison Ave., Suite 211, New York, NY 10022, tel. 212/759–1025.

Home Exchange See *Home Exchanging: A Complete Sourcebook for Travelers at Home or Abroad* by James Dearing (Globe Pequot Press, Box Q, Chester, CT 06412, tel. 800/243–0495; in CT 800/962–0973).

Getting There On international flights, children under two not occupying a seat pay 10% of adult fare. Various discounts apply to children 2–12. Reserve a seat behind the bulkhead of the plane, which offers more legroom and can usually fit a bassinet (supplied by the airline). At the same time, inquire about special children's meals or snacks, offered by most airlines. (See "TWYCH's Airline Guide," in the February 1988 issue of *Family Travel Times*, for a rundown on children's services furnished by 46 airlines.) Ask your airline in advance if you can bring aboard your child's car seat. (For the booklet "Child/Infant Safety Seats Acceptable for Use in Aircraft," write Community and Consumer Liaison Division, APA-400 Federal Aviation Administration, Washington, DC 20591, tel. 202/267–3479.)

Baby-sitting Services Child-care arrangements are easily made through your hotel concierge.

Hints for Disabled Travelers

The **Information Center for Individuals with Disabilities** (20 Park Plaza, Room 330, Boston, MA 02116, tel. 617/727–5540) offers useful problem-solving assistance, including lists of travel agents who specialize in tours for the disabled.

Moss Rehabilitation Hospital Travel Information Service (12th St. and Tabor Rd., Philadelphia, PA 19141, tel. 215/329–5715) provides information on tourist sights, transportation, and accommodations in destinations around the world. The fee is $5 for each destination. Allow one month for delivery.

Mobility International (Box 3551, Eugene, OR 97403, tel. 503/343–1284) has information on accommodations, organized study, and so forth, around the world.

The **Society for the Advancement of Travel for the Handicapped** (26 Court St., Penthouse Suite, Brooklyn, NY 11242, tel. 718/858–5483) offers access information. Annual membership is $40, or $25 for senior travelers and students. Send $1 and a stamped, self-addressed envelope.

The Itinerary (Box 1084, Bayonne, NJ 07002, tel. 201/858–3400) is a bimonthly travel magazine for the disabled.

Access to the World: A Travel Guide for the Handicapped by Louise Weiss is useful but out of date. Available from the publisher, Henry Holt & Co., tel. 212/599–7600. *Frommer's Guide for Disabled Travelers* is also useful but dated.

Hints for Older Travelers

The **American Association of Retired Persons** (AARP, 1909 K St. NW, Washington, DC 20049, tel. 202/662–4850) has two programs for independent travelers: (1) the Purchase Privilege Program, which offers discounts on hotels, airfare, car rentals, and sight-seeing; and (2) the AARP Motoring Plan, which furnishes emergency aid and trip routing information for an annual fee of $29.95 per couple. AARP members must be 50 or older. Annual dues are $5 per person or per couple.

To use an AARP or other identification card, ask for a reduced hotel rate at the time you make your reservation rather than when you check out. At restaurants, show your card to the maître d' before you're seated, because discounts may be limited to certain set menus, days, or hours. When renting a car, remember that economy cars, priced at promotional rates, may cost less than cars that are available with your ID card.

Travel Industry and Disabled Exchange (TIDE, 5435 Donna Ave., Tarzana, CA 91356, tel. 818/343–6339) is an industry-based organization with a $15 per person annual membership fee. Members receive a quarterly newsletter and information on travel agencies and tours.

National Council of Senior Citizens (925 15th St. NW, Washington, DC 20005, tel. 202/347–8800) is a nonprofit advocacy group with some 4,000 local clubs across the country. Annual membership is $10 per person or $14 per couple. Members receive a monthly newspaper with travel information and an ID card for reduced-rate hotels and car rentals.

Mature Outlook (Box 1205, Glenview, IL 60025, tel. 800/336–6330), a subsidiary of Sears, Roebuck & Co., is a travel club for people over 50, with hotel and motel discounts and a bimonthly newsletter. Annual membership is $7.50 per couple. Instant membership is available at participating Holiday Inns.

Travel Tips for Senior Citizens (U.S. Dept. of State Publication 8970, revised September 1987) is available for $1 from the Superintendent of Documents, U.S. Government Printing Office, Washington, DC 20402.

Further Reading

Mordecai Richler's *Son of a Smaller Hero* and *St. Urbain's Horseman* provide excellent descriptions of life in Montreal. Brian Moore's *The Luck of Ginger Coffey* is the story of an Irish family in Montreal. *The Main*, by Trevanian, is a suspense novel set in the underside of Montreal. *The Last Collection*, by Seymour Blicker, is a comedy about cons in the area. Roy Gabrielle's *The Tin Flute*, translated from the French, describes a poor section of Montreal called St. Henri. Other titles include Yves Beauchemin's *Le Metou*.

Getting to Montreal

By Plane

Montreal is served by two airports: **Dorval International,** 14 miles (22.5 kilometers) west of the city, handles domestic and most U.S. flights; **Mirabel International,** 34 miles (54.8 kilometers) northwest of the city, is a hub for the rest of the international trade. A direct flight makes one or more stops before its final destination; a nonstop is just that; and a connecting flight means you will have to change planes at least once en route.

The Airlines From the United States: **Air Canada** (tel. 800/422–6232) has nonstop service from New York and Miami and direct service from Boston, Chicago, Cleveland, Los Angeles, and San Francisco. **American Airlines** (tel. 800/433–7300) has nonstop service from Chicago with connections to the rest of the United States. **British Airways** (tel. 800/247–9297) has nonstop service from Detroit to Montreal. **Canadian Airlines International,** formerly CP Air (tel. 800/425–7000) has a nonstop charter from Miami and direct or connecting service from Hawaii, Los Angeles, and Pittsburgh. **Delta Air Lines** (tel. 800/843–9378) has nonstops from Boston, Hartford, Conn., and Miami and connecting service from most major U.S. cities. **Eastern Airlines** (tel. 800/327–8376) has nonstop service from New York and Philadelphia with connections to the rest of the Eastern system via Atlanta. **Piedmont Airlines** (tel. 800/241–5720) has nonstops to Montreal via Syracuse, NY. **US Air** (tel. 800/428–4322) has nonstop service from Buffalo, NY, and Pittsburgh.

From the United Kingdom: **Air Canada** (tel. 01/759–2636) has nonstop service from London into Mirabel International Airport. **British Airways** (tel. 01/759–5511) has nonstop from London with connections to most major European cities.

Flying Time   From New York, 1½ hours; from Chicago, 2 hours; from Los Angeles, 6½ hours (with a connection).

Checked Luggage   U.S. airlines allow passengers to check in two suitcases whose total dimensions (length + width + height) do not exceed 60 inches. There are no weight restrictions on these bags.

Rules governing foreign airlines vary from airline to airline, so check with your travel agent or the airline itself before you go. All airlines allow passengers to check in two bags. In general, expect the weight restriction on the two bags to be not more than 70 pounds each, and the size restriction on the first bag to be 62 inches total dimensions, and on the second bag, 55 inches total dimensions.

Carry-on Luggage   New rules have been in effect since January 1, 1988, on U.S. airlines with regard to carry-on luggage. The model for these new rules was agreed to by the airlines in December 1987 and then circulated by the Air Transport Association with the understanding that each airline would present its own version.

Under the model, passengers are limited to two carry-on bags. For a bag you wish to store under the seat, the maximum dimensions are 9″ × 14″ × 22″, a total of 45″. For bags that can be hung in a closet or on a luggage rack, the maximum dimensions are 4″ × 23″ × 45″, a total of 72″. For bags you wish to store in an overhead bin, the maximum dimensions are 10″ × 14″ × 36″, a total of 60″. Your two carry-ons must each fit one of these sets of dimensions, and any item that exceeds the specified dimensions will generally be rejected as a carry-on, and handled as checked baggage. Keep in mind that an airline can adapt these rules to circumstances, so on an especially crowded flight, don't be surprised if you are allowed only one carry-on bag.

In addition to the two carry-ons, the rules list eight items that may also be brought aboard: a handbag (pocketbook or purse), an overcoat or wrap, an umbrella, a camera, a reasonable amount of reading material, an infant bag, crutches, cane, braces, or other prosthetic device upon which the passenger is dependent, and an infant/child safety seat.

Note that these regulations are for U.S. airlines only. Foreign airlines generally allow one piece of carry-on luggage in tourist class, in addition to handbags and bags filled with duty-free goods. It is best to check with your airline ahead of time to find out the exact rules regarding carry-on luggage.

Luggage Insurance Airlines are responsible for lost or damaged property only up to $1,250 per passenger on domestic flights, up to $9.07 per pound ($20 per kilogram) for checked baggage on international flights, and up to $400 per passenger for unchecked baggage on international flights. If you're carrying valuables, either take them with you on the airplane or purchase additional insurance for lost luggage. Some airlines will issue additional luggage insurance when you check in, but many do not. One that does is American Airlines. Its additional insurance is only for domestic flights or flights to Canada. Rates are $1 for every $100 valuation, with a maximum of $400 valuation per passenger. Hand luggage is not included.

Insurance for lost, damaged, or stolen luggage is available through travel agents or directly through various insurance companies. Two that issue luggage insurance are **Tele-Trip** (tel. 800/228–9792), a subsidiary of Mutual of Omaha, and the **Travelers Insurance Co.** (tel. 800/243–0191). Tele-Trip operates sales booths at airports, and also issues insurance through travel agents. Tele-Trip will insure checked luggage for up to 180 days and for $500 to $3,000 valuation. For 1–3 days, the rate for a $500 valuation is $8.25; for 180 days, $100. The Travelers Insurance Co. will insure checked or hand luggage for $500–$2,000 valuation per person, and also for a maximum of 180 days. Rates for 1–5 days for $500 valuation are $10; for 180 days, $85. For more information, write the Travelers Insurance Co., Ticket and Travel Dept., 1 Tower Sq., Hartford, CT 06183. Both companies offer the same rates on domestic and international flights. Check the travel pages of your Sunday newspaper for the names of other companies that insure luggage. Before you go, itemize the contents of each bag in case you need to file an insurance claim. Be certain to put your address on each piece of luggage, including carry-on bags. (A business address is recommended, so thieves don't have directions to your empty house.) If your luggage is stolen and later recovered, the airline must deliver the luggage to your home free of charge.

Discount Flights The major airlines offer a range of tickets that can increase the price of any given seat by more than 300%, depending on the day of purchase. As a rule, the further in advance you buy the ticket, the less expensive it is and the greater the penalty (up to 100%) for canceling. Check with airlines for details.

It's important to distinguish between companies that sell seats on charter flights and companies that sell one of a block of tickets on scheduled airlines. Charter flights are the least expensive and the least reliable—with chronically late departures and not infrequent cancellations. They also tend to depart less frequently (usually once a week) than regularly scheduled flights. A wise alternative to a charter is a ticket on a scheduled flight purchased from a wholesaler or ticket broker. It's an unbeatable deal: a scheduled flight at up to 50% off the APEX fare. Tickets can usually be purchased up to three days before departure (but in high season expect to wait in line an hour or so).

The following brokers specialize in discount sales; all charge an annual fee of about $35–$50. **Discount Travel International** (114 Forrest Ave., Narberth, PA 19072, tel. 800/458–0503), **Moment's Notice** (40 E. 49th St., New York, NY 10017, tel. 212/486–0503), **Stand-Buys Ltd.** (311 W. Superior, Suite 414, Chicago, IL 60610, tel. 800/255–0200), **Worldwide Discount Travel Club** (1674 Meridian Ave., Miami Beach, FL 33139, tel. 305/534–2082).

Three international airlines **Aerolineas Argentinas** (tel. 800/327–0276), **Lan Chile** (tel. 800/225–5526), and **Royal Air Maroc** (tel. 800/223–5858), have weekly or biweekly flights from New York to Montreal. As of August 1988 the round-trip airfare is $100, though tickets must be purchased seven days in advance. **Air Canada** also offers a number of reduced rate fares subject to special conditions.

Enjoying the Flight If you're lucky to be able to sleep on a plane, it makes sense to fly at night. Unless you are flying from Europe or Great Britain, jet lag won't be a problem. There is little or no time difference between Montreal and most points in the United States and Canada. Sleepers usually prefer window seats to curl up against; those who like to move about the cabin should request an aisle seat. Bulkhead seats (adjacent to the "Exit" signs) have more legroom, but seat trays are attached rather awkwardly to the arms of your seat rather than to the back of the seat ahead.

Smoking If smoking bothers you, ask for a seat far away from the smoking section. If the airline tells you there are no nonsmoking seats, insist on one: DOT regulations require airlines to find seats for all nonsmokers.

From the Airports to Center City The Dorval Airport is 20 to 30 minutes from downtown Montreal, while Mirabel is about 45 minutes away.

By Taxi A taxi from Dorval to downtown will cost around $18 to $20. The taxi rates from Mirabel to the center of Montreal average between $40 and $45, and you can count on about the same cost for a taxi between the two airports. All taxi companies in Montreal must charge the same rates by law. It is best to have Canadian money with you, because the exchange rate for U.S. dollars is at the driver's discretion.

By Bus **Aerocar** (tel. 514/397–9999) provides a much cheaper alternative into town from both airports. For $7 from Dorval or $9 from Mirabel, an Aerocar van will take you into the city with stops at the Sheraton Center, the Château Champlain Hotel, the Queen Elizabeth Hotel (next to Gare Centrale), and the Voyageur bus station. Service between the two airports is $9. Aerocar buses leave Dorval every 20 minutes on weekdays and every half hour on weekends. From Mirabel buses leave hourly or every half hour between 1 PM and 7 PM.

2 Portrait of Montreal

The Voyageurs

by William Toye

"The canoes are coming!" This news, shouted in the streets of Montreal, had traveled by messenger from Lachine nine miles away. There was reason for excitement: The canoes carried furs, tons of them, and they were just a first installment from the beaver-rich far northwest. Traders had collected them, voyageurs had brought them down, and now they would be crammed into the storehouses of the new North West Company and prepared for shipment to England. The fur trade was on a scale undreamed of in the days of New France, and the Scottish, American, and English merchants who owned this company had put it there. They considered the whole northwest their province, and they had the money, the organization, and the men to make it yield its riches, be it ever so far away. They turned Montreal into a center of commerce.

There was a time when these shrewd businessmen had been merely adventurers. In their younger days the St. Lawrence system of rivers and lakes had lured them west in search of furs. They found more than they even dreamed of and this led to their own prosperity and to that of Montreal: It also led to the opening up of half a continent. The names of some of these Montrealers are part of the history of Canada—Alexander Henry, the Frobisher Brothers, William McGillivray, James McGill, and the most intrepid of them all, Alexander Mackenzie, who was the first to travel overland to the Pacific.

With the excitements of life in the Far West behind them forever, these partners in the fur trade formed a club to perpetuate their memories. They called it the Beaver Club, and it met every two weeks. Members were elected by ballot, and only those who had withstood the rigors of a winter in the Indian country could belong. A gold Beaver Club medal with a ribbon of sky blue had to be worn to every meeting on pain of a $1 fine; and no member could entertain or accept an invitation on club days. The club toasts were always the same—to the Mother of all saints; the king; the fur trade and all its branches; voyageurs' wives and children; and absent members—and only after these toasts were made could wine drinking begin.

All that went on at their dinners was done in remembrance of their rugged past (the club motto was "Fortitude in Distress"). They ate the meat of the posts—beaver, bear, and venison; they talked of their adventures, and after the calumet was passed around for each man to puff, someone would make a harangue in the fashion of the Indians. Wine drinking invariably led to the "grand voyage" when all sat on the floor as if in a huge canoe, and armed with a poker, a cane, or a sword, pretended to paddle as they tried to keep time to a voyageur's song. In 1797 Alexander Mackenzie gave a dinner for some of the Nor'west-

Reprinted from The St. Lawrence *by William Toye (Henry Z. Walck, Inc., 1959).*

ers, and though not a club affair, it was probably typical. In the small hours of the morning the wine drinking got out of hand. After the married men retired, wrote one of the guests,

We now began in right earnest and true highland style, and by four o'clock in the morning, the whole of us had arrived at such a degree of perfection that we could all give the war-whoop as well as Mackenzie and McGillivray, we could all sing admirably, we could all drink like fishes, and we all thought we could dance on the table without disturbing a single decanter, glass or plate by which it was profusely covered; but on making the experiment we discovered that it was a complete delusion, and ultimately we broke all the plates, glasses, bottles, &c. and the table also, and worse than all, the heads and hands of the party received many severe contusions, cuts, and scratches. . . .

In the meantime the wintering partners were up in the fur country trading, as the merchants themselves had long since ceased to do, and the furs were pouring into Montreal. When the first brigade arrived at Lachine in September, the road to Montreal that bypassed the rapids was crowded with ox carts trundling and squeaking with their loads of pelts. And with them were the voyageurs, each one brandishing a red paddle, some letting loose an Indian shriek in their eagerness to reach Montreal. Most of them came from river farms and would be in time to help with the harvest. But farm life was not for them. It could not give them the joy of speeding over rivers and lakes, of sending their haunting melodies over some northern wilderness; they would not have traded places with anyone when the shout *"Allumez!"* brought a brief halt to their feverish paddling and they laid down their paddles, lit their pipes, and told jokes and stories or simply lost themselves in contented silence.

Even their hardest chores seemed to give them pleasure:

Not long after leaving Lachine we reached the Ottawa River, and soon came to the foot of a tremendous rapid. Here we stopped a short time. All hands except the steersmen and bowmen of each canoe debarked, and after attaching a long tug-rope to the bow, all but the two plunged into the ice-drifting cold water and with great perseverance and risk waded up the rapid, drawing the canoe after them. They were fully half an hour before they overcame the Sault, and then the poor fellows were nearly exhausted from cold and violent exertion.

After a slight warming by a fire made for the purpose, we again embarked, and the merry song again enlivened the well-plied paddles.

Unloading for portages; trotting through bush with heavy sacks on head and back or with the rim of a canoe lying on naked shoulders; braving sudden lake squalls (a birchbark canoe is a fragile thing)—these were more of the labors and hazards of their life. But at nightfall, after supper was over and a blazing fire lit up their camp, their dancing and singing were none the less gay for the toil they had put behind them.

Sometimes they had tents, but more often their bed was a rocky beach, their shelter a half-turned canoe or nothing at all. Deaf to all night-sounds (water falling, an owl screeching), they quickly dropped off to sleep. A few hours later the cry *"Alerte!"* woke them, and they set out while it was still dark for another 15 to 18 hours of paddling and carrying, singing, smoking, and eating. There were brief revels at Michilimackinac to look forward to, and at Grand Portage, then farther west they went, and farther north.

One old voyageur, well over 70, could look back upon a lifetime spent in the Indian country and grow red-faced and breathless with excitement just telling about it:

I have now been forty-two years in this country. For twenty-four I was a light canoeman; I required but little sleep, but sometimes got less than required. No portage was too long for me; all portages were alike. My end of the canoe never touched the ground till I saw the end of it. Fifty songs a day were nothing to me. I could carry, paddle, walk, and sing with any man I ever saw. During that period I saved the lives of ten bourgeois, and was always the favourite, because when others stopped to carry at a bad spot, and lost time, I pushed on—over rapids, over cascades, over chutes; all were the same to me. No water, no weather ever stopped the paddle or the song. . . . I wanted for nothing; and I spent all my earnings in the enjoyment of pleasure. Five hundred pounds twice told have passed through my hands; although now I have not a spare shirt to my back, nor a penny to buy one. Yet were I young, I should glory in commencing the same career again. I would spend another half-century in the same fields of enjoyment. There is no life so happy as a voyageur's *life. . . .*

But it had anxieties that their ceremonies were meant to relieve. They always said a prayer in the voyageurs' chapel at the rapid of Ste-Anne, a carrying place at the end of Montreal Island where they considered their journey to begin; pulling off their caps, they said another when they passed from the St. Lawrence to the Ottawa and whenever they saw a high wooden cross near a dangerous rapid (a sign that here a voyageur had lost his life). When they wanted to summon a favorable breeze on some northern lake, they scattered tobacco on its surface, or water from their paddle blades, Indian-style. *"Souffle, souffle, la vieille!"*—"Blow, blow, old woman of the wind!" they said aloud.

The "Goers and Comers"—those voyageurs who didn't winter in the Indian country—were part of the life of the St. Lawrence. They were short, stocky men with powerful arms and shoulders; their faces were brown and leathery; their hair hung lank and long as a protection against mosquitoes. And they could sing—strong vocal cords were as necessary as strong arms. They wore a shirt and deerskin leggings; a red woolen cap (it looked like a nightcap) pierced with a feather; a blue hood; and a colored sash with a beaded pouch hanging from it. A short pipe usually stuck out of their mouths.

At the end of April the marketplace of Montreal was filled with voyageurs putting in time before leaving for the West. They drank and then they fought, and crowds collected to cheer them on. Sometimes there were a dozen fights going on at once, and whenever a man was downed, another voyageur stepped in to take his place. No one broke up the fights, for to the voyageurs they were merely good-natured feats of endurance and strength; to the people of Montreal they were a show worth watching.

They left for the north in May when the river was free. The canoes were taken empty to Lachine where they were packed with the trade goods and food that had been sent by road. All was bustle and noise on the river then, for crowds from Montreal lined the shore to see them leave. The canoes were pulled up on the beach—each one about 36 feet long, six feet wide in the middle, with prow and stern rising sharply and emblazoned with a star or a chieftain's head. Children and wives clustered round to watch some voyageurs gum the seams of their overturned canoes; others filling sacks with trade goods, collecting the pork and peas and sea biscuit that would be their food for a month; launching, loading. When all was ready, there were farewells. Then the Nor'Westers gingerly got into the canoes, pushed off from the wharf, and steered into position. They remained still for a minute. Heaped high with goods, the canoes lay low in the water; 14 canoemen in each held paddles poised; the clerks and traders sat motionless in the middle. Then a steersman gave a signal and all the red blades jabbed the water together; the brigade was off. One of the steersmen chose a song, gave the pitch, and began to sing: "*Par un matin je me suis levé/Plus matin que la lune, eh la!*" Suddenly the air was filled with a chorus of high powerful voices stressing the beat with each stroke of the paddle. They sang slowly at first, then faster and faster as they worked up to one stroke a second.

It was a cheerful song, but it sounded sad to the people on shore. It stood for long absences, for a life whose mysterious lure they knew nothing of. Hushed, they listened to the melody swell loud and strong while the canoes were still near, then fade and die away as the brigade floated off and the last canoe vanished from sight.

Around the turn of the century the North West Company sent fleets of *bateaux* to the north as well as canoes. Because they were flat, they drew only about 20 inches of water when fully loaded and could float safely over the shallows and be poled over the rapids of the Upper St. Lawrence without capsizing. In 1804 the Irish poet Thomas Moore traveled from Kingston to Montreal in a *bateau* with a crew of voyageurs. Their singing of "*M'en revenant de la Vendée*" stirred him to write "The Canadian Boat Song," which English-speaking people have ever since associated with the voyageur. Though the poet tells in the second verse of *rowing* up the Ottawa (they rowed *bateaux* only on the St. Lawrence—they *paddled* up the Ottawa in canoes), his poem captures in English the rhythm of a typical voyageur song and the spirit of their journeys:

Faintly as tolls the evening chime
Our voices keep tune and our oars keep time,
Soon as the woods on shore look dim,
We'll sing at Ste-Anne's our parting hymn,
Row, brothers, row, the stream runs fast,
The rapids are near and the daylight's past.

3 Essential Information

Arriving and Departing

By Train The Gare Centrale (Central Station) on Belmont between University and Mansfield (behind the Queen Elizabeth Hotel) is the rail terminus for all trains from the United States and other Canadian provinces. It is connected by underground passageway to the Metro's Bonaventure stop (schedule information tel. 514/871–1331).

Amtrak (tel. 800/426–8725) has daily service from New York's Grand Central Terminal, departing at 10:45 AM and arriving in Montreal at 8:01 PM (the reverse trip leaves Montreal at 9:25 AM and arrives in New York at 6:38 PM). Round-trip tickets are substantially discounted over two one-way fares, except on major holidays. There is also a special fare for married couples. At press time (summer 1988) U.S. politicians are trying to convince Amtrak to reinstate the plusher overnight Montrealer service.

VIA Rail (tel. 800/361–5390) connects Montreal by train with all the major cities of Canada, including Quebec City, Halifax, Ottawa, Toronto, Winnipeg, Calgary, and Vancouver.

By Bus **Greyhound/Trailways** has coast-to-coast service and serves Montreal with buses arriving from and departing for various cities in North America. **Vermont Transit** (tel. 800/451–3292) also serves Montreal, by way of Boston, New York, and other points in New England. Both lines use the city's primary bus terminal, Terminus Voyageur (tel. 514/842–2281), atop the Berri-UQAM Metro station in downtown.

By Car Travelers can reach Montreal by a number of well-marked highways. At the border you clear Canadian Customs, so be prepared with proof of citizenship and your vehicle's ownership papers. On holidays and during the peak summer season, expect waits of a half hour or more at the major crossings. The New York State Thruway (I-87) becomes Highway 15 at the Canadian border, and then it's 30 miles (47 kilometers) to the outskirts of Montreal. U.S. I-89 becomes Route 133, a two-land road, after the border until it hits the highway at Iberville. From I-91 you must take Highways 55 and 10 to reach Montreal.

Once you're in Quebec the road signs will be in French but marked so you shouldn't have much trouble understanding them. The speed limit is posted in kilometers; on highways the limit is 100 kph (about 62 mph). A minority of Quebec drivers like to travel much faster than posted speed limits, so beware, and take comfort that their highway patrol is after them with as much or more tenacity than state troopers in the United States. There are extremely heavy penalties for driving while intoxicated, and drivers and front seat passengers must wear over-the-shoulder seat belts. Buckle up and don't drink and drive. Gasoline is sold in Imperial gallons (equal to 1.2 U.S. gallons), and lead-free is called *sans plomb*. If you're traveling in the depths of winter, remember that your car may not start on extra cold mornings unless it has been kept in a heated garage. All Montreal parking signs are in French so brush up on your *gauche* and *droit*. And you might see more of the city if you leave your car in a garage and hop aboard Montreal's extensive, excellent rapid transit system, the Metro.

From Center City to the Airports **Aerocar** (tel. 514/397–9999) buses depart regularly from the Voyageur bus terminal at Berri-UQAM Metro station with stops at the Sheraton Center, Château Champlain, Le Grand Hotel, and the Queen Elizabeth Hotel en route to both airports ($7 to Dorval, $9 to Mirabel). Taxis can be engaged from your hotel lobby or call any of the following major taxi companies: **Champlain** (tel. 514/273–2435); **Co-op** (tel. 514/725–9885); **Diamond** (tel. 514/273–6331); **La Salle** (tel. 514/277–2552); **Veterans** (tel. 514/273–6351). Limo service to the airport can be arranged through **Contact Limousine Service** (tel. 514/631–5466) or **Murray Hill Limousine Service** (tel. 514/937–5311).

Important Addresses and Numbers

Tourist Information The **Greater Montreal Convention and Tourism Bureau's Information Center** is in Old Montreal at Place Jacques Cartier, 174 Notre Dame Street East, near the Champs de Mars Metro station. Open daily 9–6 from June 1 to Labor Day; the rest of the year weekdays 9–5. Information booths run by the tourist bureau are in both airport arrival areas (open daily 1–8 PM), and there is an information kiosk in Dorchester Square in the heart of downtown, near the Peel Metro station (open daily in the summer 9–6).

Consulates U.S. (Complete Desjardins Metro Place des Arts, tel. 514/281–1886).

U.K. (635 René Lévesque W, Metro Bonaventure, tel. 514/866–5863).

Emergencies Dialing 911 will put you through to the **police, fire,** and **ambulance.**

Doctors and Dentists The U.S. Consulate cannot recommend specific doctors and dentists but does provide a list of various specialists in the Montreal area. Call in advance (tel. 514/281–1886) to make sure the consulate is open.

Pharmacies There are pharmacies throughout the city—you might check the nearest shopping mall—and all of them carry American brand names. The Jean Coutu chain of pharmacies has a 24-hour store at 1370 Mount Royal Avenue East (tel. 514/527–8827), nearest Metro Mount Royal.

English Bookstores Not all bookstores in this bilingual city sell books in English; if the name of the store begins *libraire*, it's a good bet that it's French only. The **Coles** (1171 St. Catherine St. W and 3 other locations) and **W.H. Smith** (Central Station and 3 others) chains have stores throughout downtown. The **Paragraph Bookstore** (tel. 514/845–5811) at 2065 Mansfield, next to McGill, sells a wide selection of English books, tending toward the literary and academic. The **Double Hook** (1235A Greene, next to Westmount Square and Metro Atwater, tel. 514/932–5093) specializes in Canadian books from mostly English Canadian authors and is a good source for books about Montreal and Quebec.

Travel Agencies **American Express** (1141 de Maisonneuve St. W, tel. 514/284–3300). **Thomas Cook** (2020 University St., Suite 434, tel. 514/842–2541).

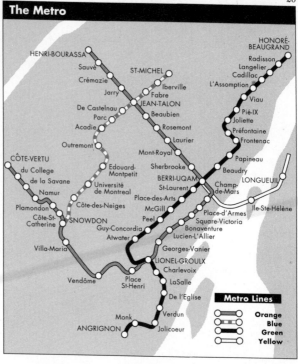

The Metro

HONORÉ-
BEAUGRAND
Radisson
Langelier
Cadillac
L'Assomption
Viau
Pié-IX
Joliette
Préfontaine
Frontenac
Papineau
Beaudry
LONGUEUIL
Champ-
de-Mars
Ile-Ste-Hélène
Place-d'Armes
Square-Victoria
Bonaventure
Lucien-L'Allier
Georges-Vanier
LIONEL-GROULX
Charlevoix
LaSalle
De l'Eglise
Verdun
Jolicoeur
ANGRIGNON
Monk
Vendôme
Place
St-Henri
Villa-Maria
Atwater
Guy-Concordia
Peel
McGill
Place-des-Arts
St-Laurent
BERRI-UQAM
Sherbrooke
Mont-Royal
Laurier
Rosemont
Beaubien
JEAN-TALON
Fabre
Iberville
ST-MICHEL
Jarry
Crémazie
Sauvé
HENRI-BOURASSA
De Castelnau
Parc
Acadie
Outremont
Edouard-
Montpetit
Université
de Montréal
Côte-des-Neiges
SNOWDON
Côte-St-
Catherine
Plamondon
Namur
de la Savane
du College
CÔTE-VERTU

Metro Lines
- Orange
- Blue
- Green
- Yellow

Getting Around

By Metro and Bus Armed with a few maps, you don't need a car to see Montreal; public transit will do quite well, thank you. The Metro is clean, quiet (it runs on rubber wheels), and safe, and it's heated in winter and cooled in summer. Metro hours are from 5:30 AM to 1 AM, and the trains run as often as every three minutes on the most crowded lines. It's also connected to the six miles (9½ kilometers) of the Underground City, so you may not need to go outside during bad weather. Each of the 65 Metro stops has been individually designed and decorated; Berri-UQAM has stained glass, and at Place des Armes are exhibited a small collection of archaeological artifacts. The recently opened stations between Snowdon and Jean-Talon on the Blue Line are worth a visit, particularly Outremont with its glass-block design. Each station connects with one or more bus routes, which cover the rest of the island. The S.T.C.U.M. (Société de transport de la Communauté urbaine de Montréal) administers both the Metro and the buses, so the same tickets and transfers are valid on either service. You should be able to go within a few blocks of anywhere in the city on one fare. Here are the 1988 rates:

One fare: $1
Six tickets: $5.50
Monthly pass: $29.75
Children: 40¢

(Conventioneers may receive a free pass called La Carte Congres good for the length of their stay.)

Free maps may be obtained at Metro ticket booths. Try to get the *Carte Réseau*, "system map"; it's the most complete. Transfers from Metro to bus are available from the dispenser just beyond the ticket booth inside the station. Bus-to-bus and bus-to-Metro transfers may be obtained from the bus driver.

By Taxi Taxis in Montreal all run on the same rate: $2 minimum and 70¢ a kilometer (at press time). They're usually prompt and reliable, although they may be hard to find on rainy nights after the Metro has closed. Each carries on its roof a white or orange plastic sign that is lit when available and off when occupied. For a list of taxi companies look in the Yellow Pages.

Staying in Touch

Telephones
Local Calls **Directory assistance** is 411 and **operator** is 0. To use a pay phone for local calls, pick up the receiver, insert 25¢, and dial the number. One quarter is good for one call of unlimited time.

International Calls To call the United States, simply dial 1, the area code, and the number. For calls to other countries, you must use the international calling system. If you want to call Britain, for example, dial 011, the country code (44), the routing code, and the number (remember the five-hour time difference).

Mail
Postal Rates International letters up to 20 grams sent outside North America need 74¢ worth of stamps, and $1.15 for letters from 20 to 50 grams. (On average, letters weigh 30 grams and postcards 15 to 20 grams). Letters up to 30 grams to the United States cost 43¢ and 63¢ for 30 to 50 grams. Mail destined within Canada costs 37¢ for up to 30 grams and 57¢ for 30 to 50 grams.

Receiving Mail American Express (tel. 514/284–3300) at 1141 de Maisonneuve W. (Metro Peel) holds mail for cardholders only (open weekdays 9–5). Thomas Cook cardholders may pick up their mail at 2020 University, Suite 434, weekdays 9–5 (tel. 514/842–2541). Mail addressed to Montreal *poste restante*, or general delivery, may be picked up at the Station A Post Office (tel. 514/283–2567) at 1025 St. Jacques (Metro Bonaventure). All post offices are open weekdays from 8 AM to 5:45 PM; Saturdays 8 AM to noon.

Opening and Closing Times

Banks are open weekdays from 10 AM to 3 PM with some banks open until 5 PM on the weekdays and open Saturday morning.

Museums are usually open during regular business hours, 9 AM to 5 PM. Check individual listings.

Shops are open generally from 10 AM to 6 PM Monday to Wednesday, 10 AM to 9 PM Thursday and Friday, 10 AM to 5 PM on Saturday. You'll find most retail stores closed on Sunday.

Tipping

Restaurants: 10–15%
Taxis: 10–15%
Porters: 50¢–75¢ a bag
Doormen: $1 for hailing a cab or carrying bags to check-in
Checkrooms: fixed fee
Ushers: no tipping expected in theaters and cinemas

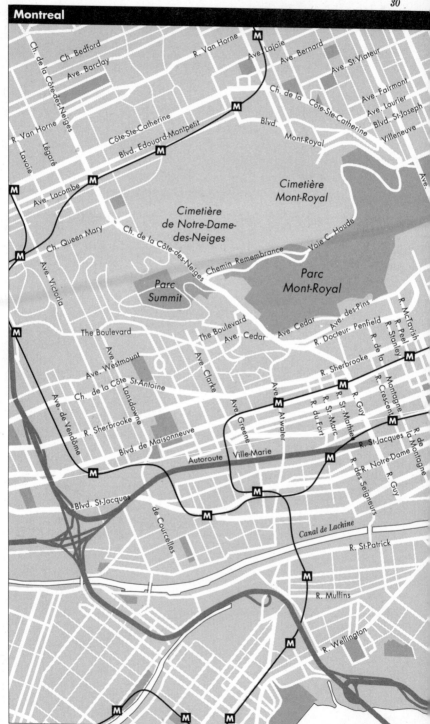

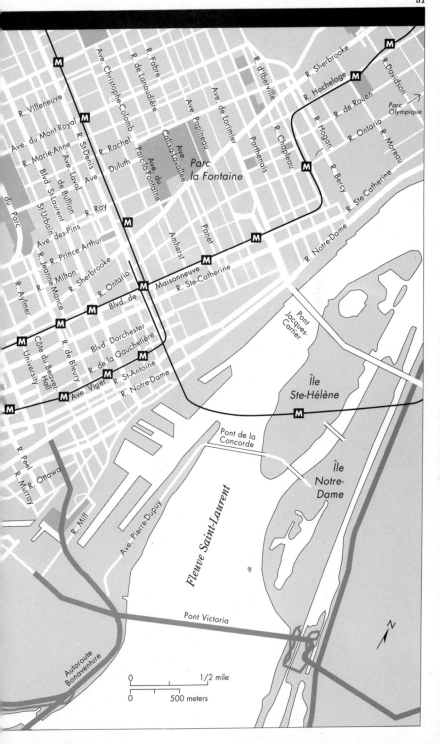

R. Villeneuve

Ave. du Mont-Royal

R. Marie-Anne

Ave. Laval

Ave. St-Denis

R. Rachel

Ave. du Parc-la-Fontaine

Ave. Duluth

Ave. Christophe-Colomb

R. de Lanaudière

R. Fabre

Ave. Papineau

Ave. de Lorimier

Ave. Calixa-Lavallée

R. d'Iberville

Parthenais

R. Chapleau

R. Sherbrooke

R. Hochelaga

R. de Rouen

R. Hogan

R. Bercy

R. Ontario

R. Moreau

R. Davidson

Parc Olympique

Parc la Fontaine

Blvd. St-Laurent

de Bullion

St-Urbain

R. Roy

Ave. des-Pins

R. Prince Arthur

R. Milton

R. Jeanne-Mance

R. Sherbrooke

R. Ontario

Amherst

Panet

Maisonneuve

R. Ste-Catherine

Blvd. de

Ave. Ste-Catherine

R. Ste-Catherine

R. Notre-Dame

du Parc

R. Aylmer

Côte du Beaver Hall

University

R. de Bleury

Blvd. Dorchester

R. de la Gauchetière

Ave. Viger

R. St-Antoine

R. Notre-Dame

Pont Jacques-Cartier

Île Ste-Hélène

R. Peel

R. Ottawa

R. Murray

R. Mill

Ave. Pierre-Dupuy

Pont de la Concorde

Île Notre-Dame

Fleuve Saint-Laurent

Pont Victoria

Autoroute Bonaventure

N

0   1/2 mile

0   500 meters

Guided Tours

Orientation Tours **Gray Line/STCUM** (tel. 514/280–5327) offer six different tours of Montreal and its environs, including St. Helen's Island, the Laurentians, and the Underground City. They offer pickup service at the major hotels, or you may board the buses at their office at 1241 Peel Street (Metro Peel).

Murray Hill (tel. 514/937–5311) offers many different tours on buses departing from Dorchester Square (Metro Peel). You may buy tickets at major hotels or from Murray Hill personnel.

Boat Tours **Montreal Harbour Cruises** (tel. 514/842–3871) offers 1½-hour tours of the harbor on the M.V. *Concordia*, an 88-foot (27-meter) ship with a restaurant, two decks, and room for 290 passengers. Boats leave as often as six times a day from Victoria Pier at the foot of Berri Street in the Old Port next to Old Montreal (Metro Champs de Mars). Also available are sunset cruises, "Moonlight" cruises, and the three-hour "Love Boat" cruise with music and dancing. The season is mid-May through September. The cruises are popular, so make reservations early (major charge cards accepted).

Amphi Tour Ltd (tel. 514/386–1298) offer short tours of the harbor that leave every 45 minutes from the Old Port.

Walking Tours The Greater Montreal Convention and Tourist Bureau Information Office at 174 Notre Dame East and Place Jacques Cartier in Old Montreal (Metro Champs de Mars) distributes a free, 31-page booklet, "A Walking Tour of Old Montreal." It is an excellent guide to Montreal's oldest and most historic quarter.

Calèche rides Open horse-drawn carriages—fleece-lined in winter—leave from Notre Dame Street between Bonsecours and Gosford streets, Dorchester Square, Place des Armes and de la Commune Street. An hour-long ride is about $30 (tel. 514/844–1313 or 845–7995).

4 Exploring Montreal

Orientation

When exploring Montreal, there's very little to remind you that it's an island. It lies in the St. Lawrence River roughly equidistant (160 miles, 256 kilometers) from Lake Ontario and the point where the river widens into a bay. For its entire length, the St. Lawrence is flanked by flat, rich bottom land for 30 miles (48 kilometers) or more on either side. The only rise in the landscape is the 764-foot (233-meter) Mount Royal, which gave Montreal its name. The island itself is 32 miles (51 kilometers) long and nine miles (14 kilometers) wide and is bounded on the north by the narrow des Prairies River and on the south by the St. Lawrence. Aside from Mount Royal, the island is relatively flat, and because the majority of attractions are clustered around this hill, tourists don't visit the rest of the island.

Head to the Mount Royal Belvedere (lookout) for a panoramic view of the city. (You can drive most of the way, park, and walk ¼ mile (½ kilometer) or hike all the way up from Côte des Neiges Ave. or des Pins Ave.) If you look directly out—southeast—from the belvedere, at the foot of the hill will be the McGill University campus and, surrounding it, the skyscrapers of downtown Montreal. Just beyond, along the banks of the St. Lawrence, are the stone houses of Vieux Montreal (Old Montreal). Hugging the opposite banks are the Îles Ste-Hélène and Notre-Dame (St. Helen and Notre-Dame islands), sites of La Ronde amusement park and Man and His World exhibition center, respectively. On a clear day you can see 40 miles (64 kilometers) or more past the river to the hills of the Eastern Townships and even to Vermont's White Mountains across the border. If you look a few degrees to the right, or due south, you may be able to make out the foothills of the Adirondacks in New York State. Closest to the mount in this direction lies the predominantly Anglophone neighborhood of Westmount with its tree-lined avenues and large, elegant houses. To the left of the belvedere are St. Louis, Plateau Mount Royal, and Terrasse Ontario, three French-flavored quarters filled with row houses, restaurants, and shops. Beyond them rises the tilted white tower of the Olympic Stadium. On the back side of Mount Royal lies Outremont, another French district, the home of the University of Montreal.

The three areas of prime interest to tourists are Old Montreal, downtown, and the French neighborhoods of St. Louis and Mount Royal. Naturally, Old Montreal is of historic importance. It also possesses some fine French restaurants alongside tourist traps, expensive shops next to souvenir stores. Downtown caters to those on the haute route who enjoying shopping in the most exclusive stores and dining in expensive restaurants. It harbors some of the city's best museums, as well as a few visit-worthy churches. St. Louis and Mount Royal exude a low-key charm and they are more residential than downtown or Old Montreal. The shops and restaurants may be expensive, but you can enjoy yourself even on a moderate budget. The street and nightlife attract a younger and more artistic crowd. There are some notable churches here, as everywhere in this city, but there are fewer edifices of historic interest. It's a place to soak in the ambience, people-watch, and relax.

There are a host of attractions that you can see on all-day and half-day trips. The most popular are the zoo, aquarium, and amusement park complex on St. Helen's Island and the Olympic Stadium and its neighbor, the Botanical Park. Often overlooked are the 500 forested acres (two square kilometers) of Mount Royal Park. Beyond the city limits are the Eastern Townships or the Laurentians for day trips or weekends in the country (*see* Excursions).

Montreal is easy to explore. Street signs, subways, and bus lines are clearly marked and the instructions usually given in both French and English. The city is divided by a grid of streets roughly aligned east-west and north-south. (This grid is tilted about 40 degrees off (to the left of) true north, so west is actually southwest and so on.) North-south street numbers begin at the St. Lawrence River and increase as you head north. East-west street numbers begin at St. Lawrence Street, which divides Montreal into east and west halves. The city is not so large that seasoned walkers can't see all the districts around the base of Mount Royal on foot.

Old Montreal (Vieux Montreal)

The St. Lawrence River was the highway on which the first settlers arrived in 1642. Just past the island of Montreal are the Lachine Rapids, a series of violent falls over which the French colonists' boats could not safely travel. It was natural for them to build their houses just above the rapids, at the site of an old Iroquois settlement on the bank of the river nearest Mount Royal. In the mid-17th century Montreal consisted of a handful of wooden houses clustered around a pair of stone buildings, the whole flimsily fortified by a wooden stockade. For the next three centuries this district—bounded by McGill and Berri streets on the east and west, St. Antoine Street on the north, and the river to the south—was the financial and political heart of the city. Government buildings, the largest church, the stock exchange, the main market, and the port were there. The narrow, but relatively straight, streets were cobblestoned and lined with solid, occasionally elegant, houses, office buildings, and warehouses, also of stone. Exiting the city meant using one of four gates through the thick stone wall that protected against Indians and marauding European powers. Montreal quickly grew past the bounds of its fortifications, however, and by World War II the center of the city had moved toward Mount Royal. The new heart of Montreal became Dominion Square. For the next two decades Old Montreal, as it became known, was gradually abandoned, the warehouses and offices emptied. In 1962 the city began studying ways to revitalize Old Montreal, and a decade of renovations and restorations began.

Today Old Montreal is a center of cultural life, if not of commerce and politics. Most of the summer activities revolve around Place Jacques Cartier, which becomes a pedestrian mall with street performers and outdoor cafés spilling out of restaurants. This lovely square is a good place to view the fireworks festival, and it's adjacent to the Old Port exhibition grounds and the docks for the harbor cruises. Classical music concerts are staged all year long at the Notre-Dame Basilica, which possesses one of the finest organs in North America, and plays are staged in English by the Centaur Theatre in the old stock exchange building. This district has six museums devoted to history, religion, decorative and fine arts, and its cobbled streets contain dozens of fine restaurants, most of them French or Quebecois. St. Paul Street is a lode of fine shops, with an emphasis on furniture, antiques, and high quality crafts, as well as tacky souvenirs. In short, Old Montreal has everything a visitor requires, except a place to rest your head (unless you count bed-and-breakfasts). The nearest hotel is the Grand at 777 University Street, to the north.

Numbers in the margin correspond with points of interest on the Old Montreal map.

To begin your tour of Old Montreal, take the Metro to the Place d'Armes station, beneath the convention center, and walk a block and a half south on St. Urbain Street to **Place d'Armes.** En route you will pass **La Presse** building, the former headquarters of North America's largest French-language newspaper. In the 1600s, Place d'Armes was the site of battles with the Iroquois and later became the center of Montreal's "Upper Town." In the middle of the square is a statue of Paul de Chomedey,

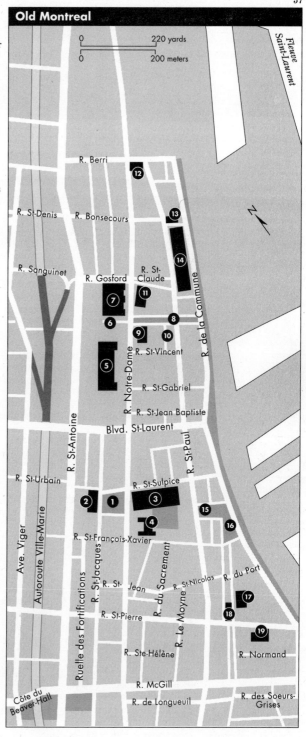

Bank of Montreal, **2**

Château Ramezay
Museum, **11**

George-Étienne Cartier
Museum, **12**

Hôtel de Ville, **7**

Marc-Aurèle Fortin
Museum, **19**

Marché Bonsecours, **14**

Montreal History
Center, **18**

Notre-Dame Basilica, **3**

Notre-Dame-de-
Bonsecours Chapel, **13**

Old Courthouse, **5**

Place d'Armes, **1**

Place Jacques Cartier, **8**

Place Royale, **15**

Place Vauquelin, **6**

Pointe-à-Callières, **16**

St. Amable Street, **10**

Sulpician Seminary, **4**

Tourist Information
Bureau, **9**

Youville Stables, **17**

Old Montreal

Fleuve Saint-Laurent

0 — 220 yards
0 — 200 meters

R. Berri

R. St-Denis

R. Bonsecours

R. Sanguinet

R. Gosford

R. St-Claude

R. de la Commune

R. St-Vincent

R. Notre-Dame

R. St-Gabriel

R. St-Jean Baptiste

Blvd. St-Laurent

R. St-Antoine

R. St-Urbain

R. St-Sulpice

R. St-Paul

Ave. Viger

Autoroute Ville-Marie

R. St-François-Xavier

R. St-Jacques

R. St- Jean

R. du Sacrement

R. St-Nicolas

R. du Port

R. St-Pierre

R. Le Moyne

Ruelle des Fortifications

R. Ste-Hélène

R. Normand

Côte du Beaver-Hall

R. McGill

R. de Longueuil

R. des Soeurs-Grises

first settlers to Montreal. In 1644 he was wounded here in a battle with 200 Indians. Historians recently uncovered a network of tunnels beneath the square; they connected the various buildings and one ran down to the river. These precursors of the Underground City protected the colonists from the extremes of winter weather and provided an escape route should the city be overrun. Unfortunately, the tunnels are too small and dangerous to visit. *Calèches*, horse-drawn carriages, are available at the south end of the square.

2 The north side of the square is dominated by the **Bank of Montreal,** an impressive building with Corinthian columns (remodeled by renowned architects McKim, Mead & White in 1905) that houses a small, interesting numismatics museum. *129 St. Jacques St. Free. Open weekdays 10–4.*

The office building to the west of the square is the site of the old Café Dillon, a famous gourmet restaurant frequented by members of the fur traders' Beaver Club (*see* Dining). Two extremely important edifices form the south end of Place d'Armes: the Sulpician Seminary, the oldest building in Montreal, and the imposing Notre-Dame Basilica.

The first church called Notre-Dame was a bark-covered structure built within the fort in 1642, the year the first settlers arrived. Three times it was torn down and rebuilt, each time in a different spot, each time larger and more ornate. The enor-
3 mous (3,800-seat) neo-Gothic **Notre-Dame Basilica,** which opened in 1829, is the most recent. The twin towers, named Temperance and Perseverance, are 227 feet (69 meters) high, and the western one holds one of North America's largest bells, the 12-ton Gros Bourdon. The interior of the church was designed in medieval style by Victor Bourgeau, with stained-glass windows, a stunning blue vaulted ceiling with gold stars, and pine and walnut wood carving in traditional Quebec style. The church has many unique features: It is rectangular rather than cruciform in shape; it faces south rather than east; the floor slopes down four feet (1¼ meters) from back to front; and it has twin rows of balconies on either side. The Casavants, a Quebec family, built the 5,722-pipe organ, one of the largest on the continent. Notre-Dame has particularly excellent acoustics and is often the site of Montreal Symphony concerts. Behind the main altar is the Sacre-Coeur Chapel, which was destroyed by fire in 1978 and rebuilt in five different styles. Also in the back of the church is a small museum of religious paintings and historical objects. *116 Notre Dame St. W, Basilica: tel. 514/ 849–1070; open 9–6. Museum: tel. 514/842–2925; admission: $1 adults, 50¢ children. Open 9:30–4:30 Fri. and Sat.*

The low, more retiring stone building behind a wall to the west
4 of the basilica is the **Sulpician Seminary.** This is Montreal's oldest building, built in 1685, and is still a residence for Sulpician monks (unfortunately closed to the public). For almost two centuries until 1854, the Sulpicians were *the* political power in the city, because they owned the property rights to the island of Montreal. They were also instrumental in recruiting and equipping colonists for New France. The building itself is the finest, most elegant example of rustic 17th-century Quebec architecture. The clock on the roof over the main doorway is the oldest (pre-1701) public timepiece in North America. Behind the seminary building is a small garden, another Montreal first.

The street that runs alongside the basilica, **St. Sulpice Street,** was the first street in Montreal. On the eastern side of the street there's a plaque marking where the Hotel-Dieu, the city's first hospital, was built in 1644. Now cross St. Sulpice Street—the Art Deco **Aldred Building** sits on the far left corner —and take Notre Dame Street East. One block farther, just past St. Lawrence Street, on the left rises the black-glass-sheathed **Palais de Justice** (1971), which houses the higher courts for both the city and the province. (Quebec's legal system is based on the Napoleonic Code for civil cases and on British common law for criminal cases.)

⑤ The large domed building at 155 Notre Dame Street East is the classic revival style **Old Courthouse** (1857), now municipal offices. Across the street at 160 Notre Dame Street East is the **Maison de la Sauvegarde** (1811), one of the oldest houses in the

⑥ city. The Old Courthouse abuts the small **Place Vauquelin,** named for the 18th-century naval hero who is memorialized by a statue in its center. North of this square is **Champs de Mars,** the former site of a colonial military parade ground but now a parking lot. The ornate building on the east side of Place

⑦ Vauquelin is the Second Empire-style **Hôtel de Ville** (city hall, 1878). On July 24, 1967, French President Charles de Gaulle stood on the central balcony of the hotel and made his famous *"Vive le Québec libre"* speech.

⑧ You are in a perfect spot to explore **Place Jacques Cartier,** the heart of Old Montreal. This two-block-long square opened in 1804 as a municipal market, and every summer it is transformed into a flower and crafts market. The 1809 monument at the top of the Place celebrates Lord Nelson's victory at Trafalgar. At the western corner of Notre-Dame Street is a small building (1811), site of the old Silver Dollar Saloon, so named because there were 350 silver dollars nailed to the floor. Today

⑨ it's the home of the **Montreal Tourist Information Bureau.** (174 Notre Dame St. E., open in summer, daily 9–6; rest of year, weekdays 9–5). Both sides of the Place are lined with two- and three-story stone buildings that were originally homes or hotels that live on today as restaurants. Two of the best eating establishments here are La Marée (*see* Dining) in the Del Vecchio House (1807), at 404 Place Jacques Cartier, and the neighboring Le St. Amable.

Time Out **Le St. Amable** (188 St. Amable St., tel. 514/866–3471) features a Businessmen's Lunch weekdays from noon–3 PM, but you don't have to be an executive or even dressed like one to sample such classics as fresh poached salmon or grilled New Zealand lamb chops.

⑩ In the summer, the one block of **St. Amable Street** becomes a marketplace for local jewelers, artists, and craftspeople. From the bottom of Place Jacques Cartier you can stroll out into the **Port of Montreal Exhibition Ground,** where from Winter Carnival through summer there is always something going on.

Retrace your steps to the north end of Place Jacques Cartier, then continue east on Notre Dame Street. At the corner of St.

⑪ Claude Street on the right is **Château Ramezay** (1705), built as the residence of the 11th governor of Montreal, Claude de Ramezay. In 1775–76 it was the headquarters for American troops seeking to conquer Canada. One of the most elegant co-

lonial buildings still standing in Montreal, the château is now a
museum, and it has been restored to the style of Governor
Ramezay's day. The ground floor is furnished like a gen-
tleman's residence of New France with dining room, bedroom,
and office. The collection includes many period artifacts, furnishings, paintings, and costumes. The basement is devoted to
displays on Indian and colonial rural life. *280 Notre-Dame E*,
*tel. 514/861–3708. Admission: $2 adults, 50¢ children. Open
Tues.–Sun. 10–4:30.*

At the end of Notre-Dame Street are two houses built by Sir
George-Étienne Cartier, a 19th-century Canadian statesman.
⑫ They recently have been opened as the **George-Étienne Cartier
Museum,** a showcase of decorative arts from colonial Quebec.
Displays depict the daily life of Montreal's elite in that era. *458
Notre-Dame St. E, tel. 514/283–2282. Admission free. Open
daily in summer 9–5; rest of the year, Wed.–Sun. 10–5.*

One block back on Notre-Dame is Bonsecours Street, one of the
oldest in the city. Turn left here, and on the left side near the
end of the block you will come upon **Les Filles du Roy** (*see* Dining), an excellent Quebecois eatery in an 18th-century house.
The neighboring building, at the corner of Bonsecours and St.
Paul Street, is the **Maison du Calvet** (1725). This fine colonial
structure was the home of Pierre du Calvet, a printer and per-
secuted sympathizer with the American Revolution. It is now a
gourmet food store. At the end of Bonsecours is the small but
⑬ beautiful **Notre-Dame-de-Bonsecours Chapel.** Marguerite
Bourgeoys, who was canonized in 1983, helped found Montreal
and dedicated this chapel to the Virgin Mary in 1657. It became
known as a sailor's church, and small wooden models of sailing
ships are suspended from the ceiling just above the congrega-
tion. The chapel also contains a crude wooden statue of the
Virgin that is said to hold a relic of St. Blaise. Bourgeoys
brought the statue from France to intensify the faith. The
chapel was twice destroyed by fire and has been renovated a
number of times, but the stained-glass windows, traditional
wood carving, and murals give the chapel a special charm. In
the basement there is a small, strange museum honoring the
saint that includes a story of her life modeled by little dolls in a
series of dioramas. A gift shop sells Marguerite Bourgeoys souvenirs. From the museum you can climb to the rather
precarious bell tower (watch the metal steps in winter) for a
fine view of Old Montreal and the port. *400 St. Paul St. E, tel.
514/656–5941. Admission: 75¢ adults, 25¢ children. Chapel
and museum open Tues.–Fri. 9–11:30 AM and 1–4:30 PM,
weekends 9–4:30.*

Double back and head west on St. Paul Street. The long, large,
⑭ domed building to the left is the **Marché Bonsecours** (1845), for
many years Montreal's main produce, meat, and fish market.
During part of the 19th century the upper floors of this neo-
Classic building were occupied by the city government—and
even for a short time by the Canadian Parliament—while the
basement was used as a market. Today the interior is not open
to the public, because, like so many other fine buildings in Old
Montreal, it has been taken over by municipal offices.

St. Paul Street is the most fashionable street in Old Montreal.
For almost 20 blocks it is lined with fine restaurants, shops, and
even a few nightclubs. Quebecois handicrafts are a specialty
here, with shops at 88, 136, and 272 St. Paul Street East. In the
basement of the **Brasserie des Fortifications,** a French restau-

rant at 262 St. Paul Street East, you can see remnants of the stone wall that once encircled Montreal. **L'Air du Temps,** at 191 St. Paul West, is the city's top jazz club. Nightly shows usually feature local talent, with occasional international name bands. Take St. Paul Street eight short blocks west of Place Jacques Cartier, and you will come to **Place Royale,** the site of the first permanent settlement in Montreal. De Maisonneuve, the city's founder, shot and killed an Iroquois chief here and later built his house across the street where 151 St. Paul Street West now stands. Place Royale was first used as a military parade ground and then became a public marketplace where, among other activities, criminals were pilloried, whipped, and hanged. Several famous duels were also fought here. The obelisk in the center of the square bears the names of the 53 first colonists on its base. At the south end of the square stands the neoclassic **Old Customs House** (1837), currently government offices. If you turn right on the next street west on St. Paul, which is St. Francois-Xavier St., you will see the **Old Stock Exchange** building (1903) at no. 453. The stock exchange occupied this fancy Beaux-Arts structure until 1965, when it moved to the new building on St. Antoine Street. It now houses the Centaur Theater, Montreal's oldest English-language playhouse.

Return to Place Royale, and behind the Old Customs House you will find **Pointe-A-Callieres,** a small park which commemorates the settlers first landing. A small stream used to flow into the St. Lawrence here, and it was on the point of land between the two waters that the colonists landed their four boats at its mouth on May 17, 1642. After they built the stockade and the first buildings at this site, it was almost washed away the next Christmas by a flood. When it was spared, de Maisonneuve placed a cross on top of Mount Royal as thanks to God. A block-and-a-half walk down William Street takes you to the **Youville Stables** on the left. These low stone buildings enclosing a garden were originally built as warehouses in 1825 (they never were stables). A group of businessmen renovated them in 1968, and the buildings now house offices, shops, and restaurants. **Gibbys** is a French-style steak and seafood restaurant in the Youville Stables. For $7–$11 a person (dinners are $20 and up) you can get a hearty lunch in their comfortable, old-French dining rooms. The stable gardens are a pleasant place for relaxation after a hard day of sightseeing. The old fire station (1906), a mix of Dutch and English styles, across William Street from the stables has become the **Montreal History Center.** Visitors to this hi-tech museum are led through a series of audio-visual environments depicting the life and history of Montreal. Small children and easily bored adults tend to fidget while enduring the rather cheesey displays. *335 St. Pierre St. Admission: $2 adults, $1 children. Open daily 10–4:30, last show begins 3:30. Closed Mon.*

Half a block to the left on St. Pierre Street is the **Marc-Aurèle Fortin Museum.** This 20th-century Canadian painter produced intense, almost visionary, landscapes of the Quebec countryside reminiscent of Van Gogh. *118 St. Pierre St. Admission: $2 adults, 75¢ children. Open 11–5 Tues.–Sun. Closed Mon.*

We now are at the end of our tour of Old Montreal. You can find the nearest Metro shop eight blocks north on McGill Street (one block west of the fire station). Or you can retrace your steps into Old Montreal and visit one of the dozens of shops, restaurants, and nightclubs.

Downtown

Downtown is a sprawling 30-by-8-block area bounded by Atwater Avenue and St. Lawernce Boulevard on the west and east respectively, des Pins Avenue on the north, and St. Antoine on the south. Two of the best museums are here, as well as fancy and cheap hotels, and hundreds of restaurants, bars, and shops catering to all tastes. It is also the financial center and the heart of the retail, fur, and fashion trades.

After 1700 Old Montreal wasn't big enough for the rapidly expanding city. In 1701 the French administration signed a peace treaty with the Iroquois, and the colonists began to feel safe about building outside Montreal's fortifications. The city inched northward, toward Mount Royal, particularly after the English conquest in 1760. By the end of the 19th century, St. Catherine Street was the main commercial thoroughfare, and the city's elite built mansions on the slope of the Mount. The area west of downtown, settled primarily by the English, became known as Westmount. (The French equivalent, Outremont, is on the far side of Mount Royal.) At that time the intersection of St. Catherine and Peel streets was considered the absolute center of the city. Since 1960 city planners have made a concerted effort to move the focus eastward. With the opening of Place des Arts (1963) and the Complexe Desjardins (1976), the city center shifted in that direction. It hasn't landed on any one corner yet, although some Montrealers will tell you it's at the intersection of de Maisonneuve and University Street.

Another major development of the last 30 years is the inauguration of the **Underground City,** an enormous network of passages linking various shopping and office complexes. These have served to keep the retail trade in the downtown area, as well as make shoppers and workers immune to the hardships of the Canadian winter. However, if you're not a fan of malls, which is after all what they are, the Underground City may hold no interest for you.

Numbers in the margin correspond with points of interest on the Downtown Montreal map.

Our tour of downtown—unless you are hale of limb you may not be able to do all of it in a day—begins at the McGill Metro station. The corner of University and de Maisonneuve Boulevard has recently been the center of intensive development. Two huge new office buildings, **2020 University** and **Galleries 2001,** with malls at street and basement levels, rise from the north side of the intersection. The southwest corner, indeed the entire block, is taken up by **Eaton,** one of the Big Three department stores in the city. Aside from many floors of mid-priced clothing and other merchandise, the real attraction of Eaton is the ninth floor Art Deco dining room.

Time Out **Eaton le 9e** was modeled after the dining room of the luxury liner *Île-de-France,* Mrs. Eaton's favorite cruise ship. Thirty-five-foot (11-meter) pink and gray marble columns hold up the ceiling, and the walls are decorated with two pre-Raphaelite murals on culinary themes. The patrons are usually shoppers, of course, dining on pasta, fish, and meat dishes. The service is

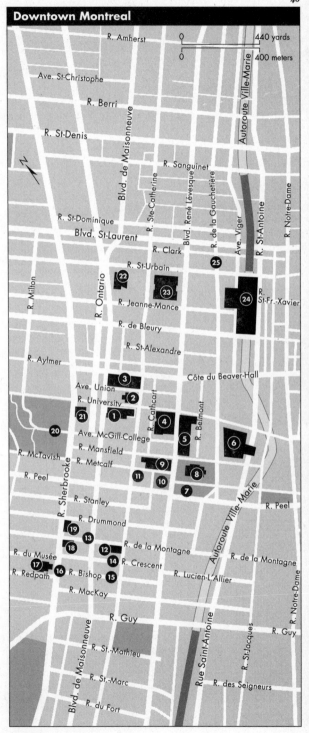

Downtown Montreal

practical and fast; the decor's the thing. *677 St. Catherine St. W, tel. 514/284–8421. AE, MC, V. Open Mon.–Wed. 11:30 AM– 5 PM, Thurs. and Fri. 11:30 AM–7 PM, Sat. 11:30 AM–4:30 PM. Closed Sun.*

Eaton is connected to **Les Terrasses** shopping complex behind it via passageways; it is connected as well to the McGill Metro and the Baie Company store.

❷ Across University Street from Eaton stands **Christ Church Cathedral** (1859), the main church of the Anglican Diocese of Montreal. In early 1988 this building was a sight. All the land beneath and surrounding the cathedral had been removed, and it was being supported solely by a number of huge steel stilts. Plagued by years of high maintenance costs and declining membership, the church fathers decided to lease their land and air rights to a consortium of developers for 99 years. The glass 34-story office tower behind the cathedral, **Le Maison des Cooperants,** and the retail complex beneath it are the products of that agreement. During the entire excavation, the stone Gothic-style structure—built in the cruciform of a 14th-century English church—has not moved an inch, and services continue uninterrupted. Behind the cathedral, at St. Cather-

❸ ine Street West and Philips Square, is **La Baie,** a branch of the nationwide chain founded in 1670 under the name Hudson's Bay Company.

Across St. Catherine Street at the corner of University and Cathcart streets is the **Tourisme Québec Information Center,** which supplies brochures, maps, and advice on what to do in the province as well as in Montreal. *2 Place Ville Marie, Suite 70, tel. 514/873–2015. Open summer 8:30 AM–8:30 PM, 9–5 rest of the year.*

❹ This entire block is **Place Ville Marie,** an office, retail, and mall complex that signaled a new era for Montreal when it opened in 1959. It was the first link in the huge chain of the Underground City, which meant that people could have access to all the services of the city without setting foot outside. It was also the first step Montreal took to claiming its place as an international city. The labyrinth that is the Underground City now includes six hotels, thousands of offices, 25 movie theaters, more than 1,000 boutiques, hundreds of restaurants, and almost eight miles (13 kilometers) of passageways in its network. It should be noted that not everyone feels this has changed Montreal for the better. Some feel that an urban mall takes people out of the hustle and bustle of the street environment and places them in a sterile, essentially lifeless enclosure that lacks any sense of community. Nevertheless, 15,000 people work in the offices at Place Ville Marie, and an estimated 75,000 people pass through its subterranean corridors every working day. The public areas are popular for brown-baggers and window-shoppers.

From Place Ville Marie head south via the passageways toward
❺ the **Queen Elizabeth Hotel.** It's easy to lose your bearings and become "lost," since directions to the next malls are not always clearly marked. (Is their intent to keep you in their own shopping area?) The Queen Elizabeth, with over 1,000 rooms, is by far the city's largest hotel (*see* Lodging). The Beaver Club (*see* Dining), named after the society of wealthy fur traders who used to meet at various gourmet restaurants, has a small muse-

um devoted to it just off the lobby. Via the underground you can reach the **Central Railway Station** just behind the hotel. Trains from the United States and the rest of Canada arrive here. Then follow the signs marked "Metro/Place Bonaventure" to **Place Bonaventure** the largest commercial building in Canada. On the lower floors there are shops and restaurants, then come exposition halls and offices, and finally the whole thing is topped by the Bonaventure Hilton International (*see* Lodging) and 2½ acres (10,100 square meters) of gardens. From here take the route marked "Place du Canada," which will bring you to the mall in the base of the **Hotel Château Champlain.** This building is known as "The Cheesegrater" because of its rows and rows of half-moon-shaped windows (*see* Lodging). Our exploration of this leg of the Underground City will end at **Windsor Station** (follow the signs). This was the second railway station built in Montreal by the Canadian Pacific Railway Company. Windsor Station was designed in 1889 by George Price, a New York architect, with a massive rustic stone exterior holding up an amazing steel and glass roof over an arcade. Soldiers departed for both World Wars here, and here, also, immigrants saw the city for the first time. The CPR planned to raze the station in the early '70s, but a citizens' protest saved it. Offices and snack bars now occupy the arcade.

It's time for a bit of fresh air now, so exit at the north end of Windsor Station and cross the street to the park known as **Place du Canada.** In the center of the park there is a statue to Sir John A. MacDonald, Canada's first Prime Minister. Then cross the park and Cathedral Street to the **Mary Queen of the World Cathedral** (1894), which you enter on René Lévesque Boulevard. This church is an exact, scale model of St. Peter's Basilica in Rome. Victor Bourgeau, the same architect who did the interior of Notre-Dame in Old Montreal, thought the idea of the cathedral's design terrible but completed it after the original architect proved incompetent. Inside there is even a canopy over the altar that is a miniature copy of Bernini's *baldacchino* in St. Peter's. The massive gray granite edifice across Fené Lévesque Boulevard from the cathedral is the **Sun Life Building** (1914), at one time the largest building in Canada. During World War II much of England's financial reserves and national treasures were stored in Sun Life's vaults. The park that faces the Sun Life building just north of René Lévesque Boulevard is **Dorchester Square,** for many years the heart of Montreal. Until 1870 a Catholic burial ground occupied this block (and there are still bodies buried beneath the grass), but with the rapid development of the area, the city fathers decided to turn it into a park. The statuary of Dorchester Square includes a monument to the Boer War in the center and a statue of the Scottish poet Robert Burns near Peel Street.

If you walk a block and a half north on Metcalf Street, the eastern boundary of Dorchester Square, you will come to the world-famous **Bens.** This glorified deli (*see* Dining) serves juicy smoked-meat sandwiches with a hefty dollop of atmosphere. It's fast and cheap and what a scene!

A block north of Dorchester Square is St. Catherine's Street, the main retail shopping street of Montreal. Three blocks west, at 1307 St. Catherine West and Mountain Street, is **Ogilvy,** the last of the Big Three department stores. The store has been divided into individual name boutiques that sell generally pricier lines than La Baie or Eaton. Most days at noon a bagpiper plays Scottish airs as he circumnavigates the ground floor. **Mountain** or **de la Montagne Street,** and **Crescent** and **Bishop** streets, the two streets just west of it, form the heart of Montreal's downtown nightlife and restaurant scene. This area once formed the playing fields of the Montreal Lacrosse and Cricket Grounds, and later it became an exclusive suburb lined with millionaires' row houses. Since then these three streets between Sherbrooke and St. Catherine streets have become fertile ground for trendy bars, restaurants, and shops ensconced in those old row houses. The **Hotel de la Montagne** at 1430 Mountain Street has a rather plain exterior, but inside it is lovingly overdecorated to something like a Baroque disco. Its restaurant, La Lutetia, is known as one of the best nouvelle cuisine eateries in the city. Crescent Street next door offers literally dozens of restaurants. Thursday's and the Winston Churchill Pub, at 1449 and 1459, respectively, are the mainstays of the Montreal bar scene.

If you walk two blocks north on Bishop Street to Sherbrooke Street, you enter a very different environment: the exclusive neighborhood known as the **Golden Square Mile.** In the 19th century this was the name of the area bounded by Guy and University streets on the east and west, on the north and south by des Pins Avenue and what is now René Lévesque Boulevard. The first wealthy inhabitants of this neighborhood were fur traders, who were followed by rail barons and other industrialists. At one time it was estimated that 70% of Canada's wealth was held by residents of the Golden Square Mile. As the commercial center edged northward after 1900, the rich moved away—either west or farther up the hill—but the area still retains its glow of opulence.

Directly across the street from the end of Bishop Street is the **Montreal Museum of Fine Arts,** the oldest established museum in Canada. The present building was completed in 1912 and holds a large collection of European and North American fine and decorative art; ancient treasures from Europe, the Near East, Asia, Africa, and America; art from Quebec and Canada; and Indian and Eskimo artifacts. From June through October there is usually one world-class exhibition, like the treasures of King Tut or the inventions of Leonardo da Vinci. The 1988– 1989 exhibition will be the works of Marc Chagall. The museum has a gift shop, an art-book store, a boutique selling Inuit art, and a gallery in which you can buy or rent original paintings by local artists. *3400 Museum Ave., tel. 514/285–1600. Admission: $6 adults, $2.50 students and senior citizens, $1 children under 12. Open Tues.–Sun. 10–7.*

Time Out The **Café du Musée** on the second floor sells a simple and inexpensive selection of soups ($1.35), quiches ($2.15), and sandwiches ($2.25–$2.95). Coffee, pastries, and the like are also available. *Open during museum hours. Dress: casual. No reservations or credit cards. Inexpensive.*

To the left of the museum, is the **Church of St. Andrew and St. Paul** with Arts and Crafts Movement-style stained glass by Sir Edward Burne-Jones and William Morris. The **Erskine and American United Church** (1893), to the museum's right, is decorated with Tiffany stained-glass windows. Walking eastward

18 on Sherbrooke Street brings you to the small and exclusive **Holt Renfrew** department store, perhaps the city's fanciest, at the corner of Mountain Street (*see* Shopping). One block farther on **19** at Drummond Street stands the **Ritz-Carlton**, the grande dame of Montreal hotels. It was built in 1912 so the local millionaires' European friends would have a suitable place to stay. Take a peek in the elegant Café de Paris restaurant. It's Montreal's biggest power dining spot, and you just might see the Prime Minister dining there. (For more on the Ritz-Carlton and its restaurants, *see* Lodging and Dining chapters). The Ritz-Carlton's only real competition in town is the modern and elegant **Hôtel Quatre Saisons** (Four Seasons), two blocks west at Sherbrooke and Peel Street. Just beyond this hotel on the other **20** side of the street begins the grassy **McGill University** campus. A wealthy Scottish fur trader, James McGill, bequeathed the money and the land for this institution, perhaps the finest English-language school of higher education in the nation, which opened in 1828. The student body numbers 15,000 and the university is best known for its medical and engineering schools. The campus is a fine place for a stroll, and during the school year you will see students and professorial types going about their rounds. The neighborhood east of the campus, the **McGill Ghetto,** was for years a haven for students living in rooming houses there, but lately professionals have been buying up the old buildings and renovating them.

The last stop on our tour of the Golden Square Mile is the **21** **McCord Museum** on Sherbrooke between Victoria and University Street. Situated in the old granite McGill Union building (1907), the McCord houses Canada's finest ethnographic collection. David Ross McCord, the museum's founder, was an early collector of Canadian Indian and Eskimo artifacts, and his collection became the core of the museum. It includes an enormous totem pole from the Pacific Northwest, which towers in the main stairwell. The costume collection is one of the largest in Canada. Every year the museum presents 10 temporary exhibitions on subjects from old toys to primitive religious art. The McCord has a small shop where are sold books and toys. *690 Sherbrooke W, tel. 514/398–7100. Admission: $1 adults, children free. Open Wed.–Sun. 11–5.*

Turn right on University Street and walk a block to the McGill Metro station. Take the train one stop in the direction of Honoré-Beaugrand to the Place des Arts station.

Montreal's Metro opened in 1966 with well-designed stations—many decorated with works of art—and modern trains running on quiet pneumatic wheels. Today there are 65 stations on four lines with 40 miles (65 kilometers) of track. The 759 train cars carry more than 700,000 passengers a day. When you exit at **22** **Place des Arts**, follow the signs to the theater complex of the same name. From here you can walk the five blocks to Old Montreal totally underground. Places des Arts, which opened in 1963, is reminiscent of New York's Lincoln Center in that it is a government-subsidized complex of three very modern theaters. The largest, Salle Wilfrid Pelletier, is the home of the Montreal Symphony Orchestra, which has won international raves under the baton of Charles Dutoit. The Grands Ballets Canadiens and the Opéra du Québec also stage productions here. At the smaller Théâtre Maisonneuve you can see less grandiose dance and theater pieces, while the smallest theater, the Théâtre Port-Royal, is devoted exclusively to drama. Large pieces of '60s-style public art are scattered throughout the theaters and lobbies. If you want to attend a performance, there's a ticket booth near the Metro entrance on the underground level. A monthly guide to upcoming events is also available here.

㉓ Next follow the signs to the **Complexe Desjardins.** Built in 1976, this is another office building, hotel, and mall development along the lines of Place Ville Marie. The luxurious Meridien Hotel (*see* Lodging) rises from its northwest corner. The large galleria space is the scene of all types of performances, from lectures on Japanese massage techniques to pop music, as well as avid shopping in the dozens of stores. The next development south is the **Complexe Guy-Favreau,** a huge federal office building named after a Quebec politician. If you continue in a **㉔** straight line, you will hit the **Montreal Convention Center** above the Place D'Armes Metro stop. But if you take a left out of Guy **㉕** Favreau onto de la Gauchetière Street, you will be in **Chinatown,** a relief after all that artificially enclosed retail space.

The Chinese first came to Montreal in large numbers after 1880 following the construction of the transcontinental railroad. They settled in an 18-block area between René Lévesque Boulevard and Viger Avenue to the north and south, by Hôtel de Ville and Bleury streets on the east and west, an area that became known as Chinatown. At its peak around 1900, there were more than 6,000 Chinese here, but a series of racist anti-immigration laws soon led to a dwindling of the population. After World War II many Chinese moved to other parts of the city and became assimilated. The last blow to Chinatown was the 1978 construction of the Complexe Guy-Favreau, which demolished 20% of the buildings and cut the neighborhood in half. In the last two years, however, there has been a revitalization of Chinatown due to the money being pumped into the community by Hong Kong investors worried about their own city's fate. If few Chinese live here, they still come to the old neighborhood on the weekend, particularly Sunday, to shop and eat in the restaurants. De la Gauchetière Street between St. Urbain Street and St. Lawrence Boulevard is Chinatown's main drag, and along it you will find many restaurants and food and gift shops. The shopping continues if you turn north on St. Laurent.

St. Denis, Prince Arthur Street, and North

After a long day of fulfilling your touristic obligations at the historical sites and museums of downtown and Old Montreal, it's good to relax and indulge in some primal pleasures, like eating, shopping, and clubbing. For these and other diversions, head to the neighborhoods east and north of downtown. Our tour begins in the Latin Quarter, the main student district, then wends its way north past some excellent restaurants, through a square that attracts many artists, over a pedestrian mall that is a center of nightlife, along a street of incredible ethnic diversity, then crosses one of the ritziest shopping streets and stops at what some consider the best bagel bakery in the world. Along the way you'll see how regular Montrealers of all ethnic backgrounds—French, English, Jewish, Portuguese—

live in blocks of row houses decorated with two-story outdoor spiral staircases.

The southern section of this area, around the base of St. Denis Street, was one of the city's first residential neighborhoods, built in the 19th century as the city burst the bounds of Old Montreal. Then known as Faubourg St. Laurent, it was the home of many wealthy families. The lands to the north of present-day Sherbrooke Street were mostly farms and limestone quarries. In 1852 much of St. Denis was destroyed by a devastating fire. As the upper class families moved north, the old mansions were subdivided and rented to the many students drawn to the area by the schools built there after 1900. The St. Louis and Plateau Mount Royal neighborhoods attracted many middle-class families in the late 19th century. After World War II many of those same families moved out to the recently opened suburbs. All these neighborhoods emptied and the housing stock deteriorated. In the mid-'60s young people began to move back to the city and buy and renovate the old houses. Since then the area has been revitalized, and a decidedly youthful air prevails.

Numbers in the margin correspond with points of interest on the St. Denis, Prince Arthur, and North map.

❶ Our tour begins at the **Berri UQAM** Metro stop, perhaps the most important in the whole city as three lines intersect here. This area, particularly along **St. Denis Street** on either side of Maisonneuve Boulevard, is known as the **Latin Quarter** and is the site of the **Université du Québec à Montreal** and a number of other educational institutions. St. Denis Street is lined with cafés, bistros, and restaurants that attract the academic crowd. On St. Catherine Street there are a number of low-rent nightclubs popular with avant-garde rock and roll types. Just west of St. Denis you find the **Cinémathèque Québecoise,** a museum and repertory movie house. For the price of one admission you can visit the permanent exhibition on the history of film-making equipment and see two movies. The museum also houses one of the largest cinematic reference libraries in the world. *335 de Maisonneuve Blvd., tel. 514/842–9763. Admission: $2. Library open weekdays 12:30–5; Museum and theater open Tues.–Sat. 6–9 PM, Sun. 2:30–4:30.*

❷ Around the corner and half a block north on St. Denis stands the 2,500-seat **Théâtre St. Denis,** the second largest auditorium in Montreal (after Salle Wilfrid Pelletier in Place des Arts). Sarah Bernhardt and numerous other famous actors have graced its stage. It currently is the main site for the summertime concerts of the International Festival of Jazz. On the next block north you see the Beaux-Arts **Bibliothèque nationale du Québec** (1915), a library that houses Quebec's official archives (1700 St. Denis; open Tues.–Sat. 9–5). Both sides of St. Denis Street north of here for a couple of miles are lined with restaurants, cafés, bookstores, and shops. If you have a lot of money and some hours set aside for dining, try **Les Mignardises** at 2035–37 St. Denis just south of Sherbrooke; it is known as the finest restaurant in Montreal (*see* Dining).

Continue north on St. Denis past Sherbrooke Street. On the right, above the Sherbrooke Metro station is the **Hôtel and Restaurant de l'Institut,** the hands-on training academy of the government *hôtelier* school (*see* Lodging). To the left is the

St. Denis, Prince Arthur, and North

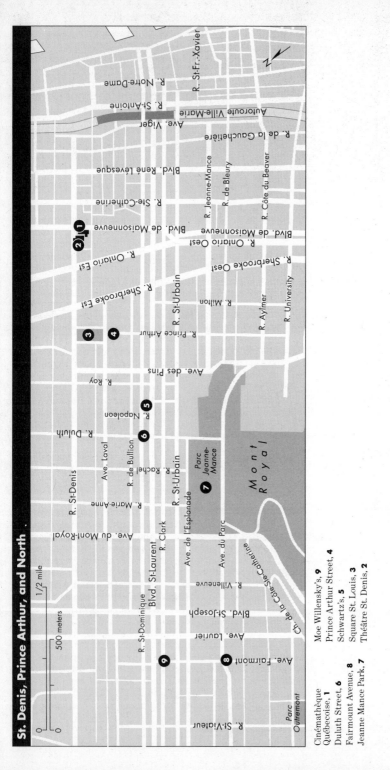

50

Cinémathèque Québecoise, **1**
Duluth Street, **6**
Fairmount Avenue, **8**
Jeanne Mance Park, **7**

Moe Willensky's, **9**
Prince Arthur Street, **4**
Schwartz's, **5**
Square St. Louis, **3**
Théâtre St. Denis, **2**

❸ small **Square St. Louis,** considered one of the most beautiful in Montreal, which gives its name to the neighborhood. Originally a reservoir, these blocks became a park in 1879 and attracted upper-middle-class families and artists to the area. French-Canadian poets were among the most famous creative people to occupy the houses back then, and the neighborhood is the home today for Montreal painters, filmmakers, musicians, and writers. On the wall of 336 Square St. Louis you can see—and read if your French is good—a long poem by Michel Bujold. Many of the houses around the park are works of art themselves; take a look at the castle roof of 357 Square St. Louis. During the winter the paths are flooded to make a skating rink, and during the summer it forms the eastern extremity of the Prince Arthur Street show.

❹ **Prince Arthur Street** begins at the western end of Square St. Louis. In the 1960s the young people moving to the neighborhood transformed the next few blocks into a mini-hippie bazaar of clothing, leather, and smokeshops. It remains a center of youth culture, although much tamer and more commercial. In 1981 the city turned the blocks between Laval Avenue and St. Lawrence Boulevard into a pedestrian mall. Hippie shops live on today as inexpensive Greek, Vietnamese, Italian, Polish, and Chinese restaurants and *boîtes* of the singles-bar variety. Every summer dozens of performers—jugglers, escape artists, musicians, mimes—take to streets, and the restaurants open terraces overlooking the show. On warm weekend nights the action can go on until daybreak. The only standout among the restaurants—they're generally mediocre—is **Pizza Mella** at 107, which serves excellent pizza with a multitude of toppings (expect a line). Most of the eateries are BYOB, but there are grocery stores as well as state liquor stores selling alcohol in the area. If you gaze up the cross streets, particularly Coloniale Avenue, you should see brightly painted houses; this is a tradition of the many recent Portuguese immigrants who live in St. Louis.

When you reach **St. Lawrence Boulevard,** take a right and stroll north on the street that cuts through Montreal life in a number of ways. First, this is the east-west dividing street; like the Greenwich Meridian, St. Lawrence is where all the numbers begin. The street is also lined with shops and restaurants that represent the incredible ethnic diversity of Montreal. Until the late 19th century this was a neighborhood first of farms and then of middle-class Anglophone residences. In 1892 was installed the first electric tramway that could climb the slope to the Mount Royal Plateau. Working-class families, who couldn't afford a horse and buggy to pull them up the hill, began to move in. In the 1880s the first of many waves of Russian-Jewish immigrants escaping the pogroms arrived and settled here. St. Lawrence Boulevard became known as "The Main," as in "main street," and Yiddish was the primary language spoken along some stretches. The Russian Jews were followed by Greeks, Eastern Europeans, Portuguese, and, most recently, Latin Americans. The next seven blocks or so are filled with delis, junk stores, restaurants, luncheonettes, and clothing stores catering to all these nationalities, but the block between Roy Street and Napoleon Street is particularly rich in delights. Just east at 74 Roy Street is **Waldman's Fish Market,** reputed to be the largest wholesale-retail fish market in North America. **Warshaw's Supermarket** at 3863 St. Lawrence is a huge Eastern

European-style emporium that sells all sorts of edible delicacies.

⑤ A few doors up the street from Warshaw's is **Schwartz's Delica-
tessen.** Among the many contenders for the smoked-meat king
title in Montreal, Schwartz's is most frequently at the top.
Smoked meat is just about all it serves, but the meat comes in
lean, medium, or fatty cuts and only costs $3 a sandwich. The
waiters give you your food and take your money and that's that.
(*See* Dining.)

⑥ A block north is **Moishe's Steakhouse** (3961 St. Lawrence
Blvd.), home of the best, but priciest, steaks in Montreal, as
well as the noisiest atmosphere. The next corner is **Duluth
Street,** where merchants are seeking to re-create Prince Arthur Street. If you take a walk to the right all the way to St.
Denis Street, you will find Greek and Vietnamese restaurants
and boutiques and art galleries on either side of the street. A
left turn on Duluth and a three-block walk brings you to
⑦ **Park Jeanne-Mance,** a flat, open field that's a perfect spot for a
picnic of delicacies purchased on The Main. The park segues
into the 494 wooded, hilly acres (two square kilometers) of
Mount Royal Park.

Park Avenue forms the western border of Park Jeanne-Mance.
To get there either cut through the park or take a left on Mount
Royal Avenue at the north end. No. 93 Mount Royal West is the
home of **Beauty's,** a kosher restaurant specializing in bagels,
lox, and omelets, i.e., breakfast. Expect a line weekend mornings. Turn right and head north on Park Avenue to see houses
with two- or three-story outdoor staircases, sometimes elabo-
rate spirals. Developers built these houses with the staircases
outdoors to save interior space during the building boom time
earlier in the century. During the winter it's cold and dangerous climbing up and down those stairs, as you can imagine, and
today it's a violation of the building code to construct such
vertigo-inducing steps. It's a five-block walk to **Laurier Avenue.** The blocks to the left on Laurier are lined with some of the
fanciest fur stores, boutiques, pastry shops, and jewelers in the
city. For a quick chocolate eclair bracer or two, go to **Lenôtre
Paris,** at 1050 Laurier, a branch of the Parisian shop of the same
name.

Time Out **La Petite Ardoise** is a casual, slightly arty café that serves
soups, quiches, sandwiches, and more-expensive daily spe-
cials. The onion soup has been lovingly overdosed with cheese,
bread, and onions. Whether it's breakfast, lunch, or dinner, the
best accompaniment for your meal is a big, steamy bowl of
creamy *café au lait*. This café is a perfect place to take a breath-
er from shopping. *222 Laurier W, tel. 514/495–4961. AE, DC,
MC, V. Open daily 8 AM–midnight, later on weekends.*

The next three blocks of Park Avenue form the heart of the
Greek district. Try **Symposium** at No. 5334 or the neighboring
Milos at 5357 Park Avenue for some of the best Greek appetizers, grilled seafood, and atmosphere you'll find in this
hemisphere.

⑧ **Fairmount Avenue,** a block north of Laurier, is the site of two
small but internationally known culinary landmarks. The
Fairmount Bagel Factory at 74 Fairmount Avenue West claims

to make the best bagels in the world. This is no small claim, and some, particularly New Yorkers, are quick to dispute it. The Shlafman family has been making bagels in this storefront since 1950 (and in Montreal since 1929). They boil the uncooked bagels in honey-sweetened water and then place them on long wooden planks and slide them into the roaring wood-fired oven. The result is a smaller, slightly cakier bagel than a classic New York bagel. The Shlafmans make all varieties of bagel, but the most popular are those smothered in sesame or poppy seeds. The Fairmount Bagel Factory is open 24 hours a day, 365 days a year. Half a block east on the corner of Fairmount and Clark Street stands the famous **Moe Willensky's Light Lunch.** Moviegoers will recognize this Montreal institution from *The Apprenticeship of Duddy Kravitz,* based on the Mordecai Richler novel of the same name. Lunch is all that's served here, and it certainly is light on the wallet. A couple of dollars will get you a hot dog or a bologna, salami, and mustard pretzel roll sandwich and a strawberry soda. Books are available for entertainment. The atmosphere is free.

From here you're on your own. You have a lot of possibilities. You can walk to St. Viateur Street, the next one north, which is the center of the Hasidic Jewish neighborhood. The *Bagel Shop* at 263 also claims to make the best bagels in the world. Or you can walk one block over to St. Laurent Street. Young fashion designers and artists have cleaned up these blocks, which used to be the kosher meat district, and turned them into a chic and arty neighborhood. In both directions you can find avant-garde boutiques, hairdressers, and some excellent restaurants, like *Prego* at 5142 St. Lawrence. Or you can return to the Metro by walking eight blocks east on Laurier Avenue (a block south) to the Laurier station.

Parks and Gardens

Of Montreal's three major parks, **Lafontaine** is the smallest (the other two are Mount Royal Park and St. Helen's Island Lafontaine Park, founded in 1867, is divided into eastern and western halves. The eastern half is French-style; the paths, gardens, and lawns are laid out in rigid geometric shapes. There are two public swimming pools on the north end along Rachel Street. In the winter the park is open for ice skating. The western half is designed on the English system, where the meandering paths and irregularly shaped ponds follow the natural contours of the topography. Rowboats can be rented for a paddle around one of two man-made lakes. It is also the site of the summer children's zoo, a kind of fanatasyland called the Garden of Wonders. Babar the Elephant, Bambi, and other storybook characters "live" there. The park also possesses the world's only statue of Tintin, the immensely popular French comic book character. With all its cut-out fairy-tale buildings, the Garden of Wonders may be too saccharine for adult tastes. Take the Metro to the Sherbrooke station and walk five blocks east along Cherrier Street. *4000 Calixa-Lavallée St., tel. 514/ 872–6211. Open mid-May–end of Sept.10 AM–sunset. Admission: $2.75 adults, $1.50 children 5–17, free under 4. (The Garden of Wonders zoo is moved to an indoor site at Angrignon Park by the Metro in the winter.)*

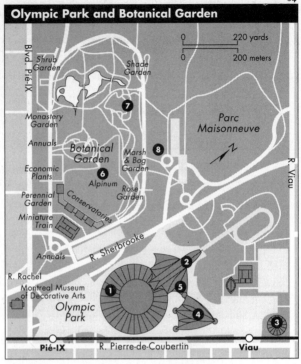

Numbers in the margin correspond with points of interest on the Olympic Park and Botanical Gardens map.

The giant mollusk-shape **Olympic Stadium** and the tilted tower that supports the roof are probably the preeminent symbols of modern Montreal. Planning for the Olympic Stadium complex began in 1972, and construction in the old Maisonneuve Park started soon afterward. The Olympics took place in 1976, but the construction still isn't finished. Montreal authorities are nevertheless proud of what they have so far. The Olympic Park includes the 70,000-seat **Olympic Stadium,** the **Tilted Tower,** six swimming pools, the **Maurice Richard Arena,** and the Olympic Village. You can tour the entire complex twice a day (at 12:30 and 2:30 PM) during the off-season, more often from May to September (tel. 514/252–4737). Anyone who delights in superlatives will not be disappointed. The guides will astound you with all the facts and figures that have been collected about the complex. During their respective seasons, of course, you can see the Expos (baseball) or Alouettes (Canadian football league). Perhaps the most popular visitor activity is a ride up to the tilted tower's observatory on the exterior cable car. The two-level cable car holds 90 people and takes two minutes to climb the 890 feet (270 meters) up to the observatory from where you can see up to 50 miles (80 kilometers) on clear days. At the **Velodrome** you can watch a bicycle race or even rent a two-wheeler, or if you've brought your swimsuit and towels, take a dip at the **Aquatic Center** (tel. 514/252–4737 for hours). There is also a cafeteria and a souvenir shop on the grounds. You can reach the **Olympic Park** via the Pie IX or Viau Metro stations (the latter is nearer the stadium entrance).

For a back-to-nature experience after all this technology, cross Sherbrooke Street to the north of the Olympic Park to reach
⑥ the **Botanical Garden** the (closest Metro stop is Pie IX). Founded in 1931 this garden is said to be one of the largest in the world. During the summer you can visit the 200 acres (809,000 square meters) of outdoor gardens—a favorite is the poisonous plants garden; the 10 greenhouses are open year-round. There are more than 26,000 species of plants here, in-
⑦ cluding notable collections of orchids, **Japanese bonsai,** begonias, and African violets. Montrealers are house-plant mad, as you can imagine with all those months of cold, so the Botanical Garden occupies a special place in the city dwellers' psyches.
⑧ During 1988 construction began on the **Insectarium,** a bug-shaped building that will house more than 50,000 insect specimens collected by the Montreal entomologist Georges Brossard. *4101 Sherbrooke St. E, tel. 514/252–1171. Greenhouse admission: $3 adults, $1.50 children. Gardens open sunrise–sunset, greenhouses 9–6.*

St. Helen's Island, opposite Old Montreal in the middle of the St. Lawrence River, draws big crowds, particularly during the warm months. You can reach it via either the Victoria or Jacques Cartier bridges, via the Metro to the Île Ste-Hélène station, or by city bus (summer only) from downtown. It's a wooded, rolling park perfect for picnicking in the summer and cross-country skiing and skating during the snow season. Originally this park was only one small island, but in the early '60s all the soil excavated during the construction of the Metro was dumped here, and it doubled in size and gained a neighbor, the Notre Dame Island. Next to the Metro stop there is a large free public pool, open in summer only (tel. 514/872–6211).

A walk along the south side of the island leads to **Château Hélène de Champlain,** a large brick mansion, now a restaurant (*see* Dining), named after the wife of the French explorer. During Expo '67 Mayor Jean Drapeau, received visiting royalty here. If you continue under the Jacques Cartier Bridge—a long, cold walk in winter—you will reach **La Ronde Amusement Park** built on the landfill from the Metro dig. La Ronde was built as part of the Expo '67 celebration. This world-class amusement park boasts a huge new roller coaster (the second-highest in the world), water slides with incredible drops, Ferris wheels, boat rides, and rides, rides, rides. To mix a little education with your sightseeing, visit the reconstructed Quebec village and Fort Edmonton on the grounds. There are also haunted houses, musical cabarets, Wild West shows, restaurants, snack bars, and the obligatory monorail and cable car rides. *St. Helen's Island tel. 514/872–6222. Admission: $15 adults, $9 children (includes all rides and entertainment), family and special Wed. rates available. Open weekends in May and early June and daily mid-June–Labor Day, noon–2:30 AM.*

Admission to La Ronde allows access to the neighboring **Alcan Aquarium.** Anyone who enjoys seeing marine life should stop in. The penguin tank is billed as the highlight, but there are also fascinating exhibits of tropical fish and local freshwater environments (see what you're having for dinner). Children (and adults who like a few chills) will enjoy looking at the poisonous lionfish, the sharks, and the enormous, grotesque South American red-tailed catfish and the 10-foot-long (3 meters) armored sturgeon. The seals perform a circus show in the summer. During the summer a bus ferries visitors from the La Ronde entrance to downtown. *Tel. 514/872–4656. Admission: $2.50 adults, $1.25 children 5–17. Open daily 10 AM–10 PM in summer, to 5 PM off-season.*

A stroll back along the north side of the island brings you to the **Old Fort** just under the Jacques Cartier Bridge. This former British arsenal has been turned into the **David M. Stewart Museum** (a museum of military history named for an historian) and a dinner-theater called **Le Festin du Gouverneur.** The latter is a re-creation of an 18th-century banquet complete with ballad-eers and comedy skits (*see* Dining). In the military museum are displays of old firearms, maps, scientific instruments, uniforms, and documents of colonial times. During the summer the parade ground is the scene of mock battles—cannons and all—by the Compagnie Franche de la Marine and bagpipe concerts by the Fraser Highlanders. *Tel. 514/861–6738. Admission: $3 adults, $2 children. Open daily 10–5, off-season closed Mon.*

From the fort you can climb the small hill at the center of the island to the **Watchtower,** from which you get a good view of the city and the St. Lawrence Seaway in the other direction. Just past the Metro station where this tour began are two small bridges to **Île Notre-Dame.** This was the site of the Olympic rowing races and most of Expo '67. The Expo pavilions still stand and are collectively called **Man and His World.** Each summer they are the site of major exhibitions. The French pavilion is now the Palais de la Civilisation, where the largest shows, like past year's Chinese and Egyptian exhibits, have been held. The enormous geodesic dome designed by Buckminster Fuller, which was the U.S. pavilion, is slated to become a science and technology museum (open during summer daily 10–10). In mid-June Notre Dame Island is the site of the Grand Prix of Canada, an auto race that inspires all quiet-loving residents within earshot to take their vacations.

The **Mount Royal Park,** the finest in the city, is easy to overlook. These 494 acres (two square kilometers) of forest and paths at the heart of the city were designed by Frederick Law Olmstead, the celebrated architect of New York's Central Park. He believed that communion with nature could cure body and soul. The park is designed following the natural topography and accentuating its features, as in the English mode. You can go skating on Beaver Lake in the winter, visit one of the three lookouts and scan the horizon, or study the park interpretation center in the chalet at the Mount Royal belvedere. Horse-drawn transport is popular year-round: sleigh rides in winter, and calèche rides in summer. On the eastern side of the hill stands the 100-foot (30-meter) steel cross that is the symbol of the city. It stands on the site where de Maisonneuve placed his famous wooden cross following the settlers' first winter. Just beyond the park on the far slopes lie two huge cemeteries of graves of many famous Montrealers. Pedestrians can climb the hill on paths beginning at the top of Peel Street and at the corner of Park Avenue and Rachel Street. Cars can climb most of the way up on roads off either Chemin de la Côtes des Neige or Mount Royal Avenue, but then you must park and finish the journey on foot.

Churches, Temples, Mosques

St. Joseph's Oratory on the northwest side of Mount Royal is a Catholic shrine on a par with Lourdes and Fatima. Take the blue Metro line to the Côte des Neiges station, then walk three blocks uphill on the Chemin de la Côte des Neiges. You can't miss the enormous church up on the hillside. Brother André, a monk in the Society of the Brothers of the Holy Cross, constructed a small chapel to St. Joseph in 1904. Brother André was credited with a number of miracles and the chapel became a pilgrimage site, the only one to St. Joseph in the world, (St. Joseph is the patron saint of healing). Inspired by the miracles and Brother André's simple, devout life, believers began sending in offerings for a shrine. The construction of the enormous basilica began in 1924 and took 31 years. The dome is among the world's largest, and while the interior is of little aesthetic interest—it resembles a blimp hangar—there is a small museum dedicated to Brother André's life, and many displays, including thousands of crutches discarded by the de-crippled faithful. Carillon and organ concerts are held weekly at the oratory, and you can still visit Brother André's original chapel at the side of the monstrous basilica. *3800 Queen Mary Rd., tel. 514/733–8211. Open daily 6 AM–10 PM.*

Harbor Cruises

If you want to see a different side of Montreal, take a harbor cruise. Boats leave from Victoria Pier at the foot of Berri Street in Old Montreal. There are as many as six daily departures. Day cruises generally last 1½ hours. Harbor cruises are popular, so call (514/842–3871) early and make a reservation.

The more adventurous might try a jet boat trip down to the Lachine rapids. In rainwear and a life jacket you roar down the river and crash through the serious rapids that stopped the first settlers' boats in the 16th century. The trip lasts 90 minutes. The specially designed jet boats leave from the same pier as the more staid cruises above. *Lachine Rapids Tours, tel. 514/284–9607. Costs: $30 per person (make reservations early). Daily summer departures 10–6.*

Off the Beaten Track

A block east of Lafontaine Park on Rachel Street stands a forgotten museum that is a must-see for those with a taste for the, well, slightly odd. The **Midget Palace** was purchased in 1913 and renovated by 36-inch-tall (92 centimeters) Phillipe Nicol, as a home for him and his wife, the "Count and Countess of Lilliputian Royalty." It was later bought by Huguette Rioux, a midget and founder of the Canadian Midgets Association, who turned it into a museum and doll hospital. On either side of the entrance are stained-glass panels depicting midgets shaking hands over the caption: Toward a New Future. Inside you can take a tour of eight rooms that have been shrunk for midget use. The doorknobs and the furniture, including a baby grand piano, have all been lowered, and the kitchen is replete with specially downsized appliances. Ms. Rioux conducts the tour. *961 Rachel E, tel. 514/527–1121. Admission: $3 adults, $2 children. Open Sun.–Thurs. 10–noon, 1–5 PM; open daily in summer, closed in Jan.*

5   Shopping

Introduction

by Patricia Lowe

Montrealers *magasiner* or go shopping with a vengeance, so it's no surprise that the city has 158 multifaceted retail areas encompassing some 5,500 stores. This rough estimate will increase substantially in 1989 when new downtown complexes will add another 680 boutiques, specialty shops, and outlets.

Visitors—especially Americans packing a strong dollar—usually reserve at least one day to hunt for either exclusive fashions along Sherbrooke Street or bargains at the Old Montreal flea market. But there are specific items that the wise shopper seeks out in Montreal.

Montreal is one of the fur capitals of the world. Close to 85% of Canada's fur manufacturers are based in the city, as are many of their retail outlets: **Alexandor** (2025 Mountain St.); **Shuchat** (2015 Mountain St.); **McComber** (440 de Maisonneuve Blvd. W); **La Baie** (Phillips Square) and **Holt Renfrew** (1300 Sherbrooke St. W) are a few of the better showrooms.

Fine English bone china, crystal, and woolens are more readily available and cheaper in metropolitan stores than in their U.S. equivalents, thanks to Canada's tariff status as a Commonwealth country. There are three **Jaeger** boutiques (Ogilvy downtown, Centre Rockland in the town of Mount Royal, and Centre Fairview in the West Island) selling traditional woolen sweaters along with $700 pure wool suits. Collectors of china and crystal will do well at any of the **Birks Jewellers** on Phillips Square or in shopping complexes and suburban shopping centers. With lower price tags, **Caplan Duval's** two branches (Côte-St-Luc's Cavendish Mall and at 6700 Côte-des-Neiges) offer an overwhelming variety of patterns.

Today, only dedicated connoisseurs can uncover real treasures in traditional pine Canadiana, but scouting around for Quebec *antiquités* and art can be fun and rewarding, especially along increasingly gentrified Notre Dame Street West.

Montreal area has five major retail districts: the city center or downtown, Old Montreal, Notre Dame Street West, the Plateau-Mount Royal-St. Denis area, and the city of Westmount.

Montreal stores, boutiques, and department stores are generally open from 9 or 9:30 to 6 Monday, Tuesday, and Wednesday. On Thursday and often on Friday, stores close at 9, Saturday at 5. A number of pharmacies are open six days a week until 11 PM or midnight, a few are 24-hour operations. Just about all stores, with the exception of some bargain outlets and a few selective art and antique galleries, accept major credit cards. Buy your Canadian money at a bank or exchange bureau beforehand to take advantage of the latest rates on the dollar.

A Quebec sales tax of 9% applies to all clothing purchases over $500 and shoes and boots over $125. There is no sales tax on books, home furnishings, or clothing sold for under $500.

If you think you might be buying fur, it is wise to check with your country's customs officials before leaving to find out which animals are considered endangered species and cannot be im-

Montreal Shopping

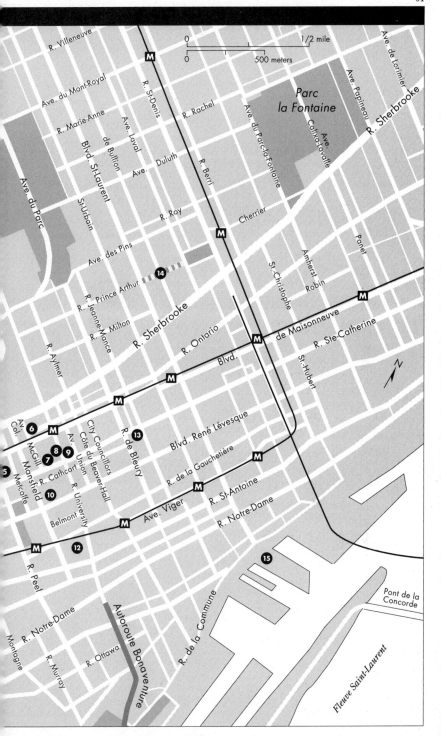

ported. Do the same if you think you might be buying Eskimo carvings, many of which are made of whalebone and ivory and cannot be brought into the United States.

City Center

Central downtown is Montreal's largest retail district. It takes in Sherbrooke Street, de Maisonneuve Boulevard, and St. Catherine Street and the side streets between them. Because of the proximity and variety of shops, it's the best shopping bet for visitors in town overnight or over a weekend.

Faubourg Ste-Catherine Several new or soon-to-open complexes have added glamour to the city center shopping scene. A good place to start is the **Faubourg Ste-Catherine,** Montreal's answer to Boston's Quincy Market. At the corner of St. Catherine Street West and Guy Street, it is a vast bazaar housed in a former parking and auto body garage abutting the Grey Nuns' convent grounds. Three levels of clothing and crafts boutiques, as well as food counters selling fruits and vegetables, pastry, baked goods, and meats, surround the central atrium of tiered fountains and islands of café tables and chairs. This is the place to pick up a $30 original Peruvian wall hanging at **Boutique Inca** or a fine French wine, also about $30, at the government-run **Société d'alcools du Québec.** Prices at most stores are generally reasonable here, especially if sampling the varied ethnic cuisine at any of the snack counters.

Les Cours Mont-Royal Continuing east on St. Catherine Street, the ultra-elegant **Les Cours Mont-Royal** dominates the east side of Peel Street between this main shopping thoroughfare and de Maisonneuve Boulevard. This mall caters to expensive tastes, but even bargain-hunters find it an intriguing spot for window-shopping. Of particular interest is the grand old Mount Royal Hotel, which fell on hard times in the 1970s and emerged in the spring of 1988 in all, if not more, of its former glory. Now it hosts such Canadian designers as Alfred Sung and his sportswear boutique, **Club Monaco.** His white marble salon is joined by boutiques like **Ferre's** sophisticated salon, **Lancia Uomo** for trendy young men, and **Aquascutum of London** for traditionalists. Montreal's popular gourmet kitchen shop, **Ma Maison,** displays splashy cookware and picnic baskets complete with flowered napkins. Le Cours' stores are temptingly arranged around a vaulted lobby with its meticulously restored pastel and gilt ceiling. Curving white stairways wend their gracious way between shopping levels while one pianist after another plays soothing selections on the central level baby grand.

Place Montreal Trust Just two blocks away, Place Montreal Trust at McGill College Avenue is the lively entrance to an imposing glass office tower. Shoppers, fooled by the aqua and pastel decor, may think they have stumbled into a California mall. Prices at the 120 outlets range from hundreds (for designs by **Alfred Sung,** haute couture at **Gigi** or **Rodier,** or men's high fashion at **Bally**), to mere dollars (for sensible cotton boys' T-shirts, or beef-and-kidney pies or minced tarts at the British dry goods and food store, **Marks & Spencer**). These imported goodies share the floor space with moderately ticketed ladies' suits, menswear, lingerie, and children's clothing. Marks and Spencer is a far cry from neighboring **Abercrombie and Fitch,** which stocks the offbeat and the outrageous, such as a fold-up miniature billiards table or a handsome $2,400 wooden rocking horse.

Soon Les Cours Mont-Royal and this complex will have competition from the **Centre Eaton** and **Promenades de la Cathèdrale.** All four of these centers will be linked to the Underground City retail network.

Always a favorite with visitors, the nearly seven-mile (11-kilometer) "city below" draws large crowds to its shop-lined corridors honeycombing between Place Ville Marie, Place Bonaventure, and Complexe Desjardins.

Place Ville Marie Weatherproof shopping began in 1962 beneath the 42-story cruciform towers of Place Ville Marie on René Lévesque Boulevard (formerly Dorchester Boulevard) at University Street. A recent renovation has opened Place Ville Marie up to the light, creating a more cheerful ambience as well as adding stores. Ville Marie's pedestrian passageways lead to such interesting specialty shops as **Le Rouet Métiers d'Art,** one of eight city branches featuring fine Quebec crafts—wood carvings and toys, hand-crafted silver jewelry, weaving, and ceramics. Souvenirs range from signed ceramic plates or wood carvings for around $50, and designer jewelry at $25, down to a scented bathcube for 29¢. The Canadian candy chain **Laura Secord** sells delicious chocolates (a box of mixed miniatures is $7) and, as in most complexes, the **Société des alcools** has an outlet here.

Stylish women head to Place Ville Marie's 85 plus retail outlets for the clothes: haute couture at **Lalla Fucci, Jacnel, Marie-Claire, Cactus,** as well as **Holt Renfrew's** branch store. More affordable clothes shops include **Dalmy's, Gazebo,** and **Reitman's** and, for shoes, **Mayfair, Brown's, François Villon,** and **Cemi.**

Place Bonaventure From here it's an easy underground trip through Gare Centrale (the train station) to Place Bonaventure's mall beneath one of Canada's largest commercial buildings. It houses some 100 stores, ranging from the trendy (**Au Coton** and **Bikini Village**) to the exclusive (**Alain Giroux** boutique) and romantic (the bridal salon **Pronuptia**). Moderately priced shoe stores abound—**Bally, Dack** and **Pegabo**—and booths on every aisle sell candy, cosmetics, and gadgets.

Complexe Desjardins Still in the downtown area but a bit farther east on René Lévesque Boulevard, is Complexe Desjardins. It's a fast ride via the Metro at Bonaventure station; just get off at Place des Arts and follow the tunnels to Desjardins' multitiered atrium mall. Also home to the Meridien Hotel, Complexe Desjardins' opening coincided with the 1976 summer Olympic Games and was an immediate hit. It is popular with a mainly French-speaking clientele, making it more typical of the city's cultural mix. Filled with splashing fountains and exotic plants, Desjardins exudes a Mediterranean *joie de vivre,* even when it's below freezing outside. Roughly 80 stores include budget outlets like **Le Château** for fashion and **Sarosi** for shoes, as well as the exclusive **Rodier of Paris,** where dresses start around $150. A pleasant art gallery, **France-Martin** on the lower level, features works by provincial and national painters.

Department Stores Still downtown, but above ground, department stores worth a browse are **La Baie, Eaton, Ogilvy,** and **Holt Renfrew** (dealing strictly in fashion). In fact, St. Catherine Street's best-shopped blocks lie between La Baie on Phillips Square and

Eaton at no. 677. Both are connected with the McGill Metro station and to even more stores in Galeries 2001 and 2020 University.

Eaton is the city's leading department store and part of Canada's largest chain. Founded in Toronto by Timothy Eaton, the first Montreal outlet appeared in 1925. It now sells everything, from the art decorating the top-floor restaurant entrance to zucchini loaves in the basement bakery. Floors in between sell Canadian crafts and souvenirs; Canadian designers like Leo Chevalier as well as labels by Nipon and Ports International; fine furnishings and accessories in addition to the bargain basement variety; microwaves, VCRs, the whole gamut of department store selections. The main restaurant is an unusual Art Deco replica of the dining room aboard the old *Île de France* ocean liner, once Lady Eaton's favorite cruise ship. Construction has begun on the $120-million Eaton Centre, which will incorporate the present store and the adjoining Les Terrasses labyrinth of boutiques.

The nearby sandstone building housing **La Baie** opened in 1891, although the original Henry Morgan Company that founded it moved to Montreal as early as 1843. Morgan's was purchased in 1960 by the Hudson Bay Company, which was founded in 1670 by famous Montreal voyageurs and trappers Radisson and Grosseilliers. For more than 150 years, Hudson Bay held the monopoly on Canada's fur trade, so it follows that this store's fur salon has a reputation for quality furs. La Baie is also known for its Hudson Bay red, green, and white-striped blankets and duffel coats. It also sells the typical department store fare.

Exclusive **Holt Renfrew,** at no. 1300 Sherbrooke Street, is also known for its furs. The city's oldest store, it was established in 1837 as Henderson, Holt and Renfrew Furriers, and made its name supplying coats to four generations of British royalty. When Queen Elizabeth II married Prince Philip in 1947, Holt's created a priceless Labrador mink as a wedding gift. Commoners, however, must be content with a brown-dyed blue fox for $14,750. The **Gucci** and **Giorgio Armani** boutiques on Holt's lower level and the elegant men's shop in a separate shop next door give a hint of the kind of prices you may expect here; even in the children's department, a size 6X velveteen dress can come to more than $200.

Around the corner and two blocks down Mountain Street, at **Ogilvy,** (1307 St. Catherine St. W) a kilted piper regales shoppers every day at noon. An institution with Montrealers since 1865, the once-homey department store has undergone a miraculous face-lift. Fortunately, it has preserved its delicate pink glass chandeliers and still stocks traditional apparel— Aquascutum, Jaeger, tweeds for men, and smocked dresses for little girls. Every Christmas its main window showcases a fantasy world of mechanized animals busy with their holiday preparations, as it has since Steiff of Germany first made the display for Ogilvy in 1947. Style-conscious clientele snap up designs by Valentino, Jean Muir, Don Sayres and Raffinati, Joan & David shoes and the unusual dyed coats in the fur salon. Crabtree & Evelyn also sells toiletries in a quaint boutique on the second floor.

This area—bounded by Sherbrooke and St. Catherine, Mountain, and Crescent streets—also boasts antiques and art galleries as well as designer salons. Sherbrooke Street is lined with an array of art and antique galleries. Notables include the **Elca London Gallery** (no. 1616), with a large collection of Eskimo and contemporary art; **Waddington & Gorce** (no. 1504), featuring contemporary pieces; the **Petit Musée** (no. 1494), selling ancient *objets* and *bijoux* from the Orient, Egypt, and Greece; **Galerie D'Art Eskimau** (no. 1434), one of the country's largest galleries specializing in Eskimo sculpture; and **Dominion Gallery** (no. 1438), known for introducing sculptor Henry Moore to Canada. Clothes horses strolling Sherbrooke stop at **Brisson & Brisson** (no. 1472), featuring elegant styles and accessories for men; **Bruestle** (no. 1490), for tailored women's classics; **Les Gamineries** (no. 1458), outfitting fashionable children; **Lily Simon** (no. 1480), for the haute couture of Armani and Valentino; **Ralph Lauren** (no. 1316), a houseful of East Coast styles; **Ungaro** (no. 1430), high fashion by a top designer; **Yves Saint Laurent** (no. 1330), the chicest salon on the street; and recent arrival **Cartier Joaillier** (at the corner of Sherbrooke and Simpson), where diamonds sparkle from showcase windows in the green marble facade.

Crescent Street is a tempting blend of antiques and fashions displayed beneath colorful awnings: **André Antiques** (no. 2125), for fine furniture, and **Ferroni** (no. 2145), known for English antiques; **Axmod** (no. 2160), featuring Cacharel and Chacok; **Celine** (no. 2142), selling crisp styles from France; and **Laura Ashley** (no. 2110), two storeys of romantic clothes, linens, and fabric.

The highly regarded **Canadian Guild of Crafts** (2025 Peel St.), between Sherbrooke Street and de Maisonneuve Boulevard, sells Inuit art and other Canadian crafts, weavings, glass, and ceramics in addition to displaying its own collection in a showroom open free of charge during business hours. Novice collectors are advised to consult guild personnel before investing in Inuit art at souvenir shops.

Old Montreal

The second major shopping district, historic Old Montreal, can be a tourist trap; but a shopping spree there can be a lot less expensive and more relaxing than shopping downtown. Both Notre Dame and St. Jacques streets, from McGill Street to Place Jacques Cartier, are lined with low- to moderately priced fashion boutiques, garish souvenir shops slung with thousands of Montreal T-shirts, and shoe stores. **Tripp Distribution & Importation** (389 and 21 Notre Dame St. W) has bargains on Ralph Lauren (polo shirts for $25) and other labels; the store prefers cash to credit cards. Quebec crafts are well represented at **Centre de Ceramique de Bonsecours** (444 St. Gabriel St.), which sells and shows ceramics and sculptures by local artisans from noon to 5. **Desmarais & Robitaille** (60 Notre. Dame St.), a store specializing in religious objects and vestments, also has lovely handcrafted souvenirs, knits, and weavings.

Cobblestoned St. Paul Street, the main historic street, has more souvenir and ice cream stands than necessary. But outdoor jewelry vendors and the range of art displayed here and along tiny St. Amable Street, off Place Jacques Cartier, make browsing fun, especially if shoppers sit for a portrait by a local caricaturist.

For finer art, go to **Galerie St-Paul** (4 St. Paul St. E), selling limited edition prints, sculptures, and works by local and international artists; or the **Guilde Graphique** (9 St. Paul St. W), for prints. **Les Artisans du Meuble Québécois** (88 St. Paul St.) has an artistic selection of Quebec-made crafts as well as silver, jewelry, and clothing. **Le Rouet,** which sells handcrafts, has its main store at 136 St. Paul Street East, while the historic **Maison du Patriote** (165 St. Paul St. E) houses a specialty candy store featuring unusual gift items. Beautiful hand-painted scarves are the only items sold at **Camelon** (161 St. Paul St. E).

Along the edge of Old Montreal is Montreal's rejuvenated waterfront, the Old Port, which hosts a sprawling flea market, the **Marché aux puces,** on Quai King Edward (King Edward Pier). Dealers and pickers search for secondhand steals and antique treasures, as they prowl through the huge hangar that is open Wednesday through Sunday from spring through early fall.

Notre Dame Street West

The place for antiquing is the city's third shopping sector, beginning at Guy Street and continuing west to Atwater Avenue (a 5-minute walk south from the Lionel-Groulx Metro station). Once a shabby strip of run-down secondhand stores, this area has blossomed beyond its former nickname of Attic Row. It now has the highest concentration of antique collectible and curiosity shops in Montreal. Collectors can find Canadian pine furniture—armoires, cabinets, spinning wheels, rocking chairs—for reasonable prices here. From Guy to Vinet Street, all outlets run along the south side of the artery; the north side is a new neighborhood of attractive brick town houses and landscaped gardens.

With rapid gentrification taking place about their ears, existing dealers have upgraded their wares, while many new shops have moved into what has become a serious shopping district. Saturday is busy, so some stores stay open on Sunday, a better day to visit as shopkeepers are more apt to offer sweeter deals.

A westbound walk along this avenue takes in: **Portes, Vitraux Anciens du Grand Montreal** (no. 1500), which sells Canadian pine furniture and stained glass; **Danielle J. Malynowsky Inc.** (no. 1640), including Victorian and Chinese pieces with Canadiana; **Marielle Moquin and Michelle Parent** (no. 1650), where silver tea services (sterling cream and sugar, $250) grace an inlaid buffet; **Martin Antiques** (no. 1730); **Antiquités Don Morton & Jean-Guy LeBlanc** (no. 1810) for Canadiana and Victoriana; **Antiquités Ambiance & Discernement** (no. 1874), blending old and new furniture designs; and **G.M. Portal Antiquités** (no. 1894), more Canadian pine. Eclectic collections (barber poles and suits of armor) crowd together at **Deuxièmement** (no. 1880). **Tendres Souvenances Antiquités** (no. 1808) has, among other things, oil lamps; and the jumbly attics of **Basilières** (no. 1904) and **Gisela's** (no. 1980) are for old dolls and teddy bears.

Plateau-Mount Royal-St. Denis

Popular with students, academics, and journalists, this east-erly neighborhood embraces St. Lawernce Boulevard, the longtime student ghetto surrounding the Prince Arthur Street mall, St. Denis Street and its Latin Quarter near the Université du Québec à Montréal campus, and the Plateau dis-trict. Plateau-Mount Royal-St. Denis attracts a trendier, more avant-garde, crowd than the determined antiquers along Notre Dame.

St. Lawrence—dubbed the Main because it divides the island of Montreal into east and west—has always been a lively com-mercial artery. It was first developed by Jewish merchants who set up shop here in the early 1900s. Cutting a broad swath across the island's center, this long boulevard has an interna-tional flavor, with its mélange of stores run by Chinese, Greeks, Slavs, Latin Americans, Portuguese, and Vietnamese immigrants. It is lined with discount clothing and bric-a-brac stores, secondhand shops, electronics outlets, and groceries selling kosher meats, Hungarian pastries, Peking duck, and natural foods. Also off this boulevard, at 74 Roy Street East, is **Waldman's** fish market, a mecca for serious cooks who delight in Gaspé salmon or *moules* (mussels). Fashionable clothing shops join this colorful bazaar though none have been as suc-cessful as the now-international **Parachute Boutique** (no. 3526), which began its career in Montreal.

While St. Lawrence personality is multiethnic, St. Denis's is distinctly French. (Both are lengthy arteries, so make use of Bus 55 for St. Lawrence, Bus 31 along St. Denis.) More aca-demic in makeup, its awnings shelter bookstores (mostly French), with **Librairie Flammarion Scorpion** (no. 4380) being one of the best. Rare and used-book stores are scattered along the street from **Librairie Kebuk** (no. 2048) to **Librairie Delteil** (no. 7348). **Archambault** (off St. Denis Street at 500 St. Cather-ine St.) caters to the city's music students. Bookstores are complemented by scattered art galleries (**Michel Tétrault**, no. 4260; **Morency**, no. 4349; **Art Select**, no. 6810) and antiques stores (**Antiquités Je Me Souviens**, no. 8271, and **Puces Libres**, no. 4240). **Le Château** has one of its many trendy fashion bou-tiques at no. 4201, and Maurice Ferland's designs are available at **Un Bien d'Elle** (no. 4417), denim sportswear by Canadian de-signers at **Revenge** (no. 3852), and international fashions at **Orphee** (no. 3997), among a wide range of other boutiques. Modern furnishings, such as colorful art clocks for $85, bright-en up the showroom at **Dixversions** (no. 4361).

Laurier Street, part of the Plateau area off Park Avenue as it climbs the mountain, is drawing a growing clientele to its cafés, boutiques, and galleries. A number of Canadian designers have based their salons on Laurier Street West: **Nikobelli** (no. 234) features Edwin Birch; **Les Tricots d'Ariane** (no. 207), for knits by Ariane Carle, and a whole raft of Canadian jewelry design-ers at **Coutu Michaud** downstairs. Pastry and chocolate are the main items at **LeNotre Paris** (no. 1050).

Westmount Square and Greene Avenue

Visitors with time to shop or friends in the elegant residential neighborhood of Westmount, a separate municipality in the middle of Montreal Island, should explore Westmount Square and adjacent Greene Avenue. Next door to downtown, these malls are on the Angrignon Metro line, easily accessible via the Atwater station, which has an exit at Westmount Square. Just follow the tunnel to this mall's 20 or so exclusive shops, including **Cacharel,** for Liberty prints; **Guy Laroche; Chacok,** for the avant-garde; **Diaghilev,** for romantic formal gowns; **Ramage** and **Victoire** of Paris. Indulgent grandmothers like the **Toy Box** and its imported dolls.

The square's plaza opens onto Greene Street two blocks long and lined with trees and flowers. Its red brick row houses and even the renovated old post office are home to a wealth of boutiques and shops. All make newcomers glad they strayed off the beaten tourist path. The food could be one reason. Costumed salespeople at the epicurean shop **By George** (no. 1343) don't mind cheering a tired nine-year-old with free samples of gingerbread while Mom settles on $5 gift boxes of maple sugar candy and a fresh *baguette*. The deli at the post office on the corner of de Maisonneuve Boulevard is always busy, as is 5 **Saisons** gourmet food store across the boulevard.

Other shops include the **Double Hook** bookstore (no. 1237), which sells works by Canadian authors only; **Coach House Antiques** (no. 1325), with fine furniture such as its Louis Philippe Semainier, circa 1875; **Connoisseur Antiques** (no. 1312), featuring china and silver. **Crisma Toys** (no. 1232) has unusual Olive Oil dolls and puppet stages both for $24, large $127 teddy bears, and a tantalizing range of items for less than $1.

6 Sports and Fitness

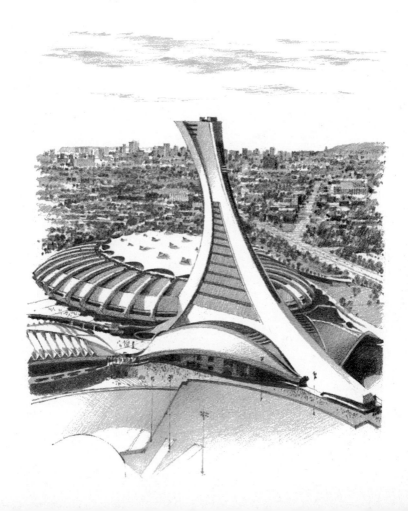

Introduction

The range of sporting activities available in Montreal is testament to Montrealers' love of the outdoors. With world-class skiing in the Laurentians less than an hour away and dozens of skating rinks within the city limits, they revel in winter. When the last snowflake has melted, they store away skis, poles, and skates and dust off their bikes, tennis rackets, and fishing poles. And year-round they watch the pros at hockey matches, baseball and football games, car races, and tennis tournaments.

Participant Sports

Bicycling The island of Montreal—except for Mount Royal itself—is quite flat, and there are more than 20 cycling paths around the metropolitan area. Among the most popular are those on St. Helen's Island, along Rachel Street, and in Maissoneuve and Mount Royal parks. You can rent 10-speeds at **Cycle Peel** (6665 St. Jacques St., tel. 514/486–1148) and **Ecole de Plein Air Dahu** (451 Maire Anne St. E, tel. 514/844–8786).

Parks Canada conducts guided cycling tours along the historic **Lachine Canal** (1825) every summer weekend. Tours leave from the corner of McGill and de la Commune streets at 10:30 AM, in English on Saturdays, in French on Sundays. For more details, call 514/283–6054. Future Olympians might want to test their skills on the angled track inside the helmet-shaped Velodrome, where the 1976 Olympic cycling events took place. Bikes and helmets are also available for rent (tel. 514/252–4737).

Curling The oldest curling club in North America—the **Royal Montreal Curling Club** (1850 de Maisonneuve Blvd. W), begun in 1807—is only one of many such organizations in the city.

Golf For a complete listing of the many golf courses in the Montreal area, call **Tourisme Quebec** at 514/873–2015. Here are some of the city's public courses:

Club de Golf de la Rive-Sud (415 Bella Vista St., Saint-Basile-le-Grand, tel. 514/653–2471).

Club de Golf Île des Soeurs (301 Golf St., Île des Soeurs, tel. 514/761–5900).

Fresh Meadows Golf Club (505 Beaconsfield Golf Ave., Beaconsfield, tel. 514/697–4036).

Health Clubs Most major hotels have pools/exercise facilities on the premises. **Club La Cité** (tel. 514/288–8221), adjacent to the Ramada Renaissance du Parc, has an indoor-outdoor pool (heated in winter), squash and tennis courts, Nautilus equipment, aerobic dance studio, sauna, whirlpool, and steamroom.

Horseback Riding For information, call **Quebec a Cheval** (tel. 514/252–3002) or the **Federation Equestre du Quebec** (tel. 514/252–3053).

Hunting and Fishing Quebec's rich waters and forests are filled with fish and wildlife. Before you begin the chase you need to purchase the appropriate license from the Ministere des Loisirs de la Chasse et de la Peche or from an authorized agent. The lakes and rivers around Montreal teem with fish, and a number of guides offer day trips. For hunting you'll have to go farther afield, to the

Laurentians or Estrie (the Eastern Townships). For complete information, call **Tourisme Quebec** (tel. 514/873–2015).

Ice Skating There are at least 30 outdoor and 23 indoors rinks in the city. You'll probably find one in the nearest park. Call parks and recreation (tel. 514/872–6211). A few of the more popular outdoor rinks include:

Angrignon Park. Night skating. 7050 de la Verendrye Boulevard.

Notre Dame Island. Olympic rowing basin.

Lafontaine Park. Parc Lafontaine Street.

Mount Royal Park. Night skating on Beaver Lake.

Jogging Montreal became a runner's city following the 1976 Olympics. There are paths in most city parks, but for running with a panoramic view, head to the dirt track in **Mount Royal Park** (take Peel street then the steps up to the track).

Rafting Montreal is the only city in the world where you can step off a downtown dock and minutes later be crashing through Class V whitewater in a sturdy aluminum jetboat. The Lachine Rapids, just south of Old Montreal, were responsible for the founding of Montreal. The roiling waves were too treacherous for the first settlers to maneuver, so they founded Ville Marie, the forerunner of Old Montreal. Modern voyageurs suit up for the 45-minute jetboat trip in multiple layers of wool and raingear, but it's nearly impossible to stay dry—or have a bad time. (Ladies, wear waterproof mascara.) **Lachine Rapids Tours Ltd.** *105 de la Commune St., Old Montreal, tel. 514/284–9607. 5 trips daily departing from Victoria Pier May–Sept. 10 AM, noon, 2, 4, and 6 PM. Trips are narrated in French and English. Rates: $30 adults; $22 children 11–18, $10 6–10; $25 senior citizens.*

Skiing With the Laurentians in their backyard, it's no surprise that skiing is the sport of choice for most Montrealers. (*See* Excursions for details on downhill and cross-country facilities in the Laurentians and Estrie.)

Alpine For the big slopes you'll have to go northwest to the Laurentians or south to the Eastern Townships, an hour or two away by car. There is a small slope in Mount Royal Park. Pick up the Ski-Quebec brochure at the Tourisme Quebec offices.

Nordic Trails crisscross most of the city's parks, including Notre Dame and St. Helen's islands, Angrignon, Maisonneuve, and Mount Royal.

Squash You can reserve court time for this fast-pace racquet sport at **Nautilus Centre de Conditionnement** (8305 Cote de Liesse Rd., tel. 514/739–3654) and **Ville-Marie Squash** (1200 McGill College Ave., Suite 300, tel. 514/861–6705).

Swimming There is a large indoor pool at the **Olympic Park** (Metro Viau, tel. 514/252–4622) and another at the **Complexe Claude-Robillard** (1000 Emile Journault, tel. 514/872–6900). The free outdoor pool on St. Helen's Island is an extremely popular (and crowded) summer gathering place. Open June–Labor Day.

Tennis There are public courts in the Jeanne Mance, Kent, Lafontaine, and Somerled parks. For details call Montreal Sports and Recreation (tel. 514/872–6211).

Windsurfing and Sailing Sailboards and small sailboats can be rented at **L'Ecole de Voile de Lachine** (2105 St. Joseph, Lachine, tel. 514/634–4326) and the **Man and His World Sailing School** (Notre Dame Island, tel. 514/872–6093)

Spectator Sports

Baseball The National League **Montreal Expos** play at the Olympic Stadium from April through September. For information, call 514/253–3434; for credit card reservations, call 514/253–0700.

Football The **Alouettes,** of the Canadian Football League, hit the Olympic Stadium gridiron from July to November (tel. 514/252–1052).

Grand Prix The annual **Canadian Grand Prix,** which draws top Formula 1 racers from around the world, takes place every June at the Gilles-Villeneuve racetrack on Notre Dame Island (tel. 514/871–1421).

Harness Racing **Hippodrome Blue Bonnets.** 7440 Decane Blvd. (Metro Namur), tel. 514/739–2741. Admission: $3–$4. Open Wednesday–Monday.

Hockey The Montreal **Canadiens,** winner of 22 Stanley Cups, meet National Hockey League rivals at the Forum (2313 St. Catherine St. W, tel. 514/932–6131) from October to April.

Marathon More than 12,000 runners do the grueling 26.2-mile **Montreal International Marathon** each September through the streets of Montreal (tel. 514/879–1027).

Tennis The **Canadian tennis championships** are held during the last two weeks of August on the courts of Jarry Park (Jarry St. and St. Lawrence Blvd., tel. 514/273–1515). The men compete in odd years, the women in even years.

7 Dining

Introduction

The promise of a good meal is easily satisfied in Montreal. Les
Montrealais don't "eat out"; they "dine." And they are passion-
ate about dining. The city has more than 5,000 restaurants of
every price representing more than 20 ethnic groups. It has
culinary institutions like Les Mignardises, Le Paris, and the
Beaver Club, which emphasize classic cuisine and tradition.
Smoked meat places such as Ben's, Briskets, and Schwartz's
are mainstays for budget dining. In between there are ethnic
eateries featuring the foods of China, Greece, India, Morocco,
and Italy. Then there are the ubiquitous inexpensive fast-food
outlets and coffee shops. The challenge to dining in Montreal is
choosing from among the thousands of restaurants and the varieties of cuisine.

Places to dine or catch a bite are scattered throughout every
neighborhood of Montreal. The most famous area—Restaurant
Row—is Crescent Street (and the neighboring Bishop and
Mountain streets) between René Lévesque Boulevard and
Sherbrooke Street. Dozens of eateries of all types of cuisine
line both sides of the street. Both St. Lawrence Boulevard and
St. Denis Street from St. Antoine Street (near Old Montreal)
north for several miles are chock-full of various types of restaurants and coffee houses. The former tends to have the cheaper,
more ethnic eateries, while along St. Denis Street can be found
more Francophile and chic cafés and cookeries. If you want to
eat the best Chinese food in town, head to Chinatown between
Viger Avenue and René Lévesque Boulevard, east of the convention center. Prince Arthur Street and Duluth Avenue, in
certain stretches, are pedestrian malls lined with ethnic, mostly Greek and Vietnamese, restaurants. Old Montreal has both
high-class French and second-class tourist eateries. By law, all
restaurants must post their menus outside, so you can window
shop for your dining spot.

Many expensive French and Continental restaurants offer two
options, which can be a blessing or a burden to your wallet. Either choice guarantees you a great meal. Instead of ordering *à
la carte*—you select each dish—you can opt for the *table d'hôte*
or the *menu de dégustation*. The *table d'hôte* is a complete two-
to four-course meal chosen by the chef. It is less expensive than
a complete meal ordered *à la carte* and often offers interesting
special dishes. It also may take less time to prepare. If you
want to splurge with your time and money, indulge yourself
with the *menu de dégustation*, a five- to seven-course dinner
executed by the chef. It usually includes, in this order, salad,
soup, a fish dish, sherbet, a meat dish, dessert, and coffee or
tea. At the city's finest restaurants, this *menu* and a good bottle of wine for two can cost $170 and last two hours. But it's
worth every cent and every second.

At the low end of the price spectrum, budget restaurants are
everywhere in Montreal. You can get a satisfying meal at the
ubiquitous sandwich-souvlaki-spaghetti-pizza establishments
or some delicious baked goods, *café au lait*, and salads at the
many *croissanteries*. American fast-food spots—Burger King,
McDonalds, Kentucky Fried Chicken, etc.—are hard to miss.
Another option is Quebec's own, home-grown chains like St.
Hubert (BBQ chicken) or Marie Antoinette (like HoJos). Excel-

lent meat and produce is available if you want to buy your own food. Surprisingly, a wide variety of tropical fruits and vegetables are sold at relatively low prices.

Montreal restaurants are refreshingly relaxed. Though only a few of the fanciest restaurants require a jacket and tie, neatness (no torn T-shirts and scruffy jeans) is appreciated elsewhere. Lunch hour is generally from noon to 2:30 PM and dinner from 6 to 11 PM or midnight. (Montrealers like to dine late, particularly on summer weekends.) Many restaurants serve dinner only on weekends. Since there is no consistent annual closing among Montreal eateries—some will take time off in August, while others will close around Christmas and January—call ahead to avoid disappointment. The following credit card abbreviations are used: AE, American Express; CB, Carte Blanche, DC; Diners Club; MC, MasterCard; and V, Visa.

The most highly recommended restaurants in each price category are indicated by a star ★ .

Category	Cost*
Very Expensive	over $30
Expensive	$20–$30
Moderate	$10–$20
Inexpensive	$5–$10

per person without tax (10% for meals over $3.25), service, or drinks

Chinese

Moderate **Cathay Restaurant.** Hong Kong investors, fearful of their city's future, are pouring money into Montreal's and other Chinatowns in North America. Among other businesses, they're opening slick, Hong Kong-style restaurants and competing with the older Chinese eateries. The consumer wins in these restaurant wars. The 15-year-old Cathay was remodeled and expanded in 1985, and is now the most popular and largest *dim sum* restaurant in the city. The two floors are both huge rooms with institutional dropped ceilings and the usual red and gold Chinese stage decorations. From 11 AM to 2:30 PM waitresses emerge from the kitchen pushing carts laden with steaming beef dumplings in bamboo steamers, spicy cuttlefish, shrimp rice noodles, bean curd rolls, and on and on. You point to what you want. Each plate costs between $1.40 and $2.25. At the end of the meal a waiter tallies your empty plates and presents you with the bill, which is usually very reasonable considering the amount of food you eat. The more crowded the restaurant is— Sunday mornings are the busiest—the greater the variety of dim sum. In the evening a standard Chinese menu is served. Wine, cocktails, and a number of Polynesian drinks, including something called à Go Go Loco (rum and coconut, $5.25) are available. *73 de la Gauchetière St. W, Chinatown, tel. 514/866-3131. Dress: informal. No reservations, so be prepared to wait on Sun. morning. AE, DC, MC, V.*
Restaurant Gourmet de Chine. Soothing is the word for this small Shanghai- and Szechuan-style restaurant near Metro

Montreal Dining

R. Villeneuve

R. du Mont-Royal

R. Marie-Anne

Ave. Laval

de Bullion

Ave. Duluth

Blvd. St-Laurent

St-Urbain

R. St-Denis

R. Rachel

R. Berri

Ave. du Parc-la-Fontaine

Ave. Calix-d-tavaille

Ave. Papineau

R. Sherbrooke

Ave. de Lorimier

Parc la Fontaine

0   1/2 mile
0   500 meters

R. Roy

Cherrier

St-Christophe

Robin

Amherst

Panet

Ave. du Parc

Ave. des Pins

R. Prince Arthur

R. Jeanne-Mance

R. Milton

R. Sherbrooke

R. Ontario

Blvd.

de Maisonneuve

R. Ste-Catherine

St-Hubert

R. Aylmer

McGill Col.

Metcalf

Mansfield

City Councillors

Côte du Beaver-Hall

Ave. Union

R. Cathcart

R. de Bleury

R. University

Blvd. René Lévesque

R. de la Gauchetière

R. St-Antoine

R. Notre-Dame

Ave. Viger

R. St-Fr-Xavier

Belmont

R. de la Commune

Autoroute Bonaventure

la

Montagne

R. Peel

R. Murray

R. Ottawa

Pont de la Concorde

Fleuve Saint-Laurent

Guy. The walls are a creamy off-white; Chinese music faintly tinkles in the background; serene Oriental landscapes decorate the walls; and fish float in large aquaria. Tuxedoed waiters provide impeccable, Continental service—they spoon the dish onto your plate rather than bang it on the table and leave. The tiny, steamed *bao* (round dumplings, $4.20) are artistic marvels, perfectly formed little sculptures of thin, chewy dough surrounding a center of spicy ground pork. Entrées like the Buddha vegetables (mixed vegetables and tofu, $5.80), are pleasing to the eye but a bit bland. Main dishes run from $5 to $11, and appetizers are $2.50 to $5. The bartender has invented a cooling, slightly bitter drink called an Oriental cocktail ($3), which is a pale pink mixture of rose liqueur, gin, vermouth, citron, and lychee nut juice. *1809 St. Catherine St. W, tel. 514/ 937–7418. Dress: informal. Reservations generally not necessary. AE, MC, V.*

Continental

Expensive **L'Intercontinental.** If you want to eat at the Ritz-Carlton, and the prices or the heady atmosphere of the Café de Paris turn you off, try one of the two downstairs restaurants. All three are served by the same kitchen, so the quality is always high. L'Intercontinental features French, Italian, and English food in three rooms, each decorated in the style of one of the countries. One meal can include a mini-European tour: smoked salmon ($7.75), vichyssoise (cold, creamy potato and leek soup, $3), and linguine bolognese ($6). There's also a cold buffet and salad menu for the diet-conscious. Service is attentive and there is a large and excellent wine cellar. *1228 Sherbrooke St. W, tel. 514/842–4212. Jackets required, no jeans. Reservations advised. AE, DC, MC, V.*

Delicatessens

Inexpensive **Bens.** Red food, they say, is happy food. If so, then Bens is a
★ bundle of joy. On the menu of this large, efficient, and charming deli, all the items with "Bens" in the name are red or are covered in red. "Ben's cheesecake" ($3.45) is smothered in strawberries; "Bens Ice Cold Drink" ($1) is the color of electric cherry juice; and the specialty, the "Big Ben Sandwich" ($6.15), is two slices of rye bread enclosing a seductive, pink pile of juicy smoked meat (Montreal's version of corned beef). According to Ben slore, the founder, Ben Kravitz, brought the first smoked-meat sandwich to Montreal in 1908. The rest, as they say, is history. A number of the walls are devoted to photos of celebrities who have visited Bens. The decor is strictly '50s, with yellow and green walls and vaguely deco, institutional furniture. Bens's waiters are often wisecracking characters but nonetheless incredibly efficient. Beer, wine, and cocktails are served. Bens's motto: "But for life the Universe were nothing, and all that has life requires nourishment." *990 de Maisonneuve Blvd. W, downtown, tel. 514/844–1000. Dress: informal. No reservations. No credit cards. Closed Sun.*

Briskets. The second of Montreal's smoked-meat triumvirate is done up in neo-student-hangout-style—old advertising posters and college banners on the walls and thick wood tables for carving your initials—appropriate decor for the location since it's next to Concordia University. Briskets serves a variety of burgers and sandwiches, but the emphasis is on smoked meat, lean, medium, and fatty. Lean is too dry and flaky, fatty is just that. So medium is the way to go: tender and juicy. A "king-size" ($6.25) sandwich is served with fat, red, pickled peppers, a slightly sweet, crisp slaw, and a sour dill pickle. There is also steak ($9.95) with sides of fries, onion rings, and "Munchy Mushrooms" ($4.25). Briskets serves draft beer and house wine but no harder stuff. The service is fast, and takeout is available. *2055 Bishop St., near Metro Guy, tel. 514/843–3650. Dress: informal. No reservations. AE, MC, V.*

Schwartz's. There's intense competition for the title as the best smoked-meat restaurant in Montreal. Briskets and Schwartz's seem to bobble the crown between themselves. Schwartz's is definitely the more traditional of the two. It occupies a storefront in the heart of the Main, the old Jewish section, and inside there's a short counter and seven or eight rows of tables. The kitchen serves up smoked-meat sandwiches ($3), steak, liver steak, frankfurters, and pickled pimento peppers. That's it. Like Briskets, the choices are lean, medium, and fatty, and the medium is the best ("Only a fool would order rare," say Schwartz's owners). The meat is more peppery on the outside than the offerings of other smoked-meat eateries, and as tender as any inside. The service is fast, if unadorned. *3895 St. Lawrence St., near Metro Mt. Royal, tel. 514/842–4813. Dress: informal. No reservations, no alcohol, no credit cards.*

French

Very Expensive **The Beaver Club.** Early fur traders started the Beaver Club in a shack during Montreal's colonial days. In the 19th century it became a social club for the city's business and political elite. It still has the august atmosphere of a men's club devoted to those who trap: pelts of bear, raccoon, and beaver still line the walls and members' engraved brass plates gleam from a sideboard near the entrance. The Beaver Club is a gourmet French restaurant open to anyone with a reservation who arrives in the proper attire. Master chef Edward Merard was among the first to introduce nouvelle cuisine to Montreal, and he has a large and devoted following. The luncheon *table d'hôte* ($16–$25) includes such dishes as terrine of duckling with pistachios and onion-and-cranberry compote. For more mundane tastes, the restaurant also specializes in meaty dishes like roast prime rib of beef *au jus* ($24.75). The Beaver Club always offers one or two low-fat, low-salt, and low-calorie plates. The waiters are veteran to the point of being antiques and the service is as excellent as the food. *The Queen Elizabeth Hotel, 900 René Lévesque Blvd. W, downtown, tel. 514/861–3511. Jacket and tie. Reservations a must. AE, DC, MC, V.*

La Marée. As you enter the old stone building on Place Jacques Cartier (in the heart of Old Montreal), which houses La Marée, you're welcomed with a plate of smoked salmon and a prosciutto surrounded by capers, onions, lemons, and other condiments. The maître d' (if you have a reservation) will then guide you into one of three intimate rooms with stone or paneled walls decorated with paintings of food and fishing boats. Classic French seafood describes the menu; the smoked salmon is a natural for an appetizer. One specialty is Pale D'Homard, lobster steamed with white wine, fresh tomato, and basil ($24), and another is veal *a l'orange* (veal scallops with orange sauce

and a perfume of tarragon, $21). The waiters specialize in
flambéeing dishes at your table. The standout dessert is the
crêpes with Grand Marnier in a copper pan at tableside. The
menu is overhauled in January and June to account for the
changing availability of various fresh seafoods. Although the
food is French, the clientele is mostly local Anglophones. The
wine list is excellent. *404 Place Jacques Cartier, Old Montreal,
tel. 514/861–8126. Dress: informal but no jeans or T-shirts.
Reservations required. AE, CB, DC, MC, V.*

★ **Le Café de Paris.** This restaurant is a masterpiece of atmosphere and of cuisine. You sit at large, well-spaced tables in a
room ablaze with flowers with the light streaming in the
French windows. During the summer you can sit outside under
a canopy and dine beside a flower-filled garden and a pool complemented with ducks. Inside or outside the waiters provide
perfect, unobtrusive service. The menu opens with a selection
of fresh caviar flown in from Petrossian in New York City. Then
you turn to the seven-course *menu de dégustation ($55)*, a meal
of small, exquisite dishes, such as quail salad with grapes, that
add up to a sumptuous repast. If you can't spend a couple of
hours over dinner, you can choose from classics like calf sweetbreads with a slightly bitter endive sauce ($21) or the flambéed
fillet of buffalo with green peppercorns ($31). At meal's end the
waiter will trundle over the dessert cart; the *crème brulée* with
raisins is a favorite. The wine list includes everything from rea-
sonably priced bottles to extremely expensive vintages. The
table to the right rear of the dining room as you enter is where
the Prime Minister dines when he's in town. If he's not there,
you are likely to see other national political and financial figures supping or schmoozing between tables. There's no place
anywhere like Le Café de Paris. *Ritz-Carlton Hotel, 1228 Sherbrooke St. W, tel. 514/842–4212. Jacket and tie required at
lunch and dinner. Reservations required. AE, DC, MC, V.*

Le Castillon. The main dining room of the very modern Bonaventure Hilton International, Le Castillon aims for the
baronial look with antique chandeliers, *faux* Renaissance tapestries, and burgundy velvet armchairs. The large windows
look out on the 17th floor gardens and ponds (with ducks, just
like the Ritz-Carlton). The cuisine is a little less *nouvelle* and
more *haute* than Le Café de Paris. Le Castillon specializes in
fresh salmon prepared in pastry with a spinach and lobster
cream sauce ($20.50) or poached with leeks and served with a
watercress sauce ($21.50). The three-course, 55-minute execu-
tive's lunch, a prompt gourmet meal for those on a schedule, is
extremely popular. Sunday night Le Castillon presents a special "Gypsy Evening" menu of Russian and Eastern European
dishes like caviar with blinis ($34.50), borscht ($4.25), and
chicken Kiev ($18.50). Once or twice a year a master French
chef does a three-week stint in its kitchen. He prepares his own
menu, and gourmands flock in to partake of his creations. Expect professional service from waiters in 17th-century French
costume and a large wine list. *Bonaventure Hilton International, 1 Place Bonaventure, downtown, tel. 514/878–
2332. Jacket and tie required. Reservations required. AE, DC,
MC, V.*

★ **Les Mignardises.** Chef Jean-Pierre Monnet used to run the
kitchen at Les Halles, Montreal's very traditional, very classic
French restaurant. Now that he has his own place, his talents
are given free range. Les Mignardises is considered the finest

and certainly the most expensive restaurant in town. You enter via the bar and climb up one flight to the simple, elegant dining room decorated with copper pans hanging from the exposed brick walls. The dining area only holds about 20 tables, so reservations are a must. If your wallet is full, you can choose the seven-course *menu de dégustation* ($58.95, or $71.50 if you allow the chef to choose the dishes for you). But if you're on a budget, it's still possible to enjoy a full meal. The three-course *table d'hôte* lunch menu ($15 or $26.75) allows you to sample delicious dishes like fish salad on gazpacho or marinated duck breast with vinegar sauce. The latter is sliced rare duck breast artfully arranged on a bed of oyster mushrooms with a slightly sweet vinegar sauce. The former is an appetizer of marinated raw salmon, tuna, and swordfish with tarragon and pink peppercorns on a light tomato gazpacho. Delicious potatoes sautéed with bouillon and onions in a little copper pot accompany the dishes. One of the house special desserts is crêpes with honey ice cream ($9.25). The presentation always takes a backseat to the taste. As you would expect, the wine list is large and pricey (the least expensive bottle is $21.50). The waiters and waitresses are prompt, knowledgeable, and friendly. *2035–37 St. Denis St., near Berri and Sherbrooke metros, tel. 514/842–1151. Dress: informal, but no jeans or T-shirts. Reservations required. AE, CB, DC, MC, V. Closed Sun. and Mon.*

Expensive– Very Expensive **Le Restaurant.** The Four Seasons' management claims to have invented Montreal's version of "power" dining here. (The competition with the Ritz-Carlton continues.) Le Restaurant certainly has the "power" look. The choicest seats are on a raised circular platform, encircled by a white Hellenistic colonnade. They are comfortable, but very businesslike, executive chairs. In these impressive surroundings Quebec's political and business leaders dine on first-class, light nouvelle cuisine. Many must suffer from high blood pressure, because the menu features "alternative cuisine," dishes with reduced salt, cholesterol, and calories. The fricassee of sweetbreads and prawns with lobster butter ($26) is not on this list. If you suffer from chronic low wallet weight, you can stop in for lunch and have the $3.50 onion soup with a ham-and-cheese sandwich on French bread for $5.50. "Power" breakfasts start at 7 AM. The standard of service here, as in the rest of the hotel, is high. The wine list is expensive and excellent, of course. *The Four Seasons, 1050 Sherbrooke St. W, tel. 514/284–1110. Jacket and tie required. Reservations required. AE, CB, DC, MC, V.*

Expensive **Auberge le Vieux St. Gabriel.** Established in a big stone house in 1754, this restaurant claims to be the oldest in America. The interior is lined with rough stone walls, and enormous old beams hold up the ceilings. In late 1987 it reopened with new owners who plan to expand both the menu and the dining space. At this writing the fare was hearty yet unadventurous French, with a bit of local Quebecois flavor. The pea soup à la Canadienne ($2.75) is yellow and chunky rather than the American-style bland green purée. The perch fillets sautéed in dill butter ($12.50) are morsels of tender fish on top of mushy, overly rich creamed mushrooms. Other entrées include beef tenderloin with morels in a brandy and cream sauce ($18.50) and a terrine of rabbit with prunes and apples in a honey cream ($14.50). If you're worried about your cholesterol, watch out. Waitresses in colonial costumes provide prompt service. The restaurant seats close to 500 people, but you'd never guess it because there are so many separate dining rooms. *426 St. Gabriel St., Old Montreal, tel. 514/878–3561. Dress: informal. Reservations suggested. AE, DC, MC, V.*

Restaurant Hélène de Champlain. Named after the wife of French explorer Samuel de Champlain, this brick chateau was where Mayor Jean Drapeau received visiting heads-of-state during Expo '67. The interior is divided into five or six richly decorated dining rooms, some with fireplaces that are invitingly ablaze in the cold months. The cuisine is classic French: snails in a pastry shell ($6.25), doré (walleye) almandine ($12.50), and rack of lamb with Dijon sauce ($18.50). The service and wine list are adequate but nothing special. The restaurant is popular for receptions and, during the all-too-brief summer, a quiet, green escape from the city. The stunning rose garden outside the rear dining room is its most famous feature. The Hélène de Champlain is about 200 yards (180 meters) from the Metro stop on St. Helen's Island (follow the signs). It can be reached by car via the Jacques Cartier and Concordia bridges. *200 Tour de St. Helen's Island, tel. 514/ 395–2424. Jacket and tie required. Reservations suggested. AE, CB, DC, MC, V.*

Moderate–Expensive **Chez Antoine.** On the lobby level of Le Grand Hotel, Chez Antoine resembles a turn-of-the-century, Art Nouveau-style bistro. The dark paneled walls are decorated with mildly risqué paintings and posters in that flowing, colorful style. The menu is divided in two. The first is a normal bistro menu of soups ($4–$5), sandwiches ($7.50–$10.50), salads ($3–$16.50), and pastas ($6–$7.50). The second half is a bit more trendy: a selection of meat and fish grilled over mesquite, hickory, sassafras, maple, and apple woods and served with one of 19 different sauces. Prices run from $12.75 for chicken to grilled prawns with curry for $26.75. Good service matches the good wine list. *Le Grand Hotel, 777 University St., downtown, tel. 514/879–1370. Dress: informal. Reservations suggested. AE, DC, MC, V.*

★ **Le Paris.** This is a true bistro, where old Francophone couples dressed to the nines sit side by side on red banquettes, sip *vin rouge*, and fork down the *choucroute garnie* (sausages and ham on a huge mound of sauerkraut, $15—a hearty meal on a winter's night). The decor is tacky French; the walls are hung with old theater posters and maritime scenes by pseudo-Impressionists, but the fare is simple, relatively inexpensive, and excellent. They serve steak grilled, with Bordelaise sauce, or *au poivre* ($17); fresh skate with *beurre noir*; and salmon poached with *beurre blanc* ($17). Desserts include praline cake ($3) and rhubarb compote, cooked in syrup ($3.50). The surroundings are homey and comfortable, unless you're near the kitchen door, which swings open every 10 seconds. *1812 St. Catherine St. W, one block from Metro Guy, tel. 514/937–4898. Dress: informal but neat. Reservations suggested. AE, MC, V. Closed Sun.*

Greek

Expensive **Milos.** Nets, ropes, floats, and lanterns—the usual tacky symbols of the sea—hang from Milos's walls and ceilings. The real display, however, is in the refrigerated cases and on the beds of ice in the back by the kitchen: fresh fish from all over the world; octopus, squid, and shrimp; crabs, oysters, and sea urchins; lamb chops, steaks, and chicken; and vegetables, cheese, and olives. In short, all the makings of your meal are there for you to inspect before you make your choice. The seafood is flown in from wholesalers in Nova Scotia, New York, Florida, and Athens. A meal can start out with chewy, tender, and hot octopus ($9.75), or if you're adventurous, you might try the cool and creamy roe scooped from raw sea urchins. The main dish at Milos is usually fish—pick whatever looks freshest—grilled over charcoal and seasoned with parsley, capers, and lemon juice. It's done to a turn and achingly delicious. The fish are priced by the pound, and you can order one larger fish to serve two or more. Don't be afraid to use your fingers: hot towels are provided at the end. The bountiful Greek salad (enough for two, $7) is a perfect side dish or can be a meal itself. For dessert you might try a *loukoumad* (honey ball, $6.50), a deep-fried puff of dough doused in honey, chopped nuts, and cinnamon. The waiters are professional but not always knowledgeable about the whole array of exotic seafood available. Milos is a healthy walk from Metro Laurier. You can also take bus 51 from the same Metro stop and ask the driver to let you off at Park Avenue; Milos is halfway up the block to the right. *5357 Park Ave., off St. Lawrence Blvd., tel. 514/272-3522. Dress: informal. Reservations required. AE, V. No lunch weekends.*

Moderate **Chez Nassos.** This Greek restaurant specializes in fish—porgy, sea and striped bass, red snapper, and salmon ($12.50–$14.75) —split open, grilled over charcoal, then coated with a light, garlicky lemon sauce and a sprinkling of capers. The meat melts away in your mouth, and at meal's end you may find yourself scraping the bones for the last morsels. The appetizers include spinach pie ($3.75) and tarama (fish roe, $3.25). The baklava ($1.75), the classic Greek dessert, is too doughy—the phyllo isn't crisp—and it could use an extra dollop of honey. You can wash down the fish with a bottle of Greek wine ($13 and up). Chez Nassos's interior is green and white, and stained-glass panels with fish motifs hang from the walls. *5115 St. Lawrence Blvd., 6 blocks from Metro Laurier, tel. 514/276-2719. Dress: informal. Reservations rarely necessary. AE, MC, V. No lunch.*

Indian

Inexpensive **Pique-Assiette.** The name of this popular Indian restaurant means "spicy dish." For under $10 you can get a complete, tasty meal that includes meat, rice, vegetable and a *rig nan*, a large flat loaf of warm and chewy bread. Half of a chicken prepared *tandoori*-style is a reasonable $7.95. The kitchen will prepare the curry hot or mild as you like it, but if it's too spicy try the *lassi*, a yogurt, mint, and soda water shake ($1.75). They also serve a few humdrum dishes like onion soup ($2.75) and hamburgers. The decor is halfway to a fast-food restaurant: exposed brick, ceiling fans, metal chairs, and a skylight over the back room. If you're on the way to a hockey match at the nearby Forum, the service is prompt and friendly. Pique-Assiette is part of the Bombay Palace international chain of Indian restaurants and hotels. *2051 St. Catherine St. W, near Metro Guy, tel. 514/932-7141. Dress: informal. Reservations not required. AE, DC, MC, V.*

Italian

Expensive **Prego.** European chic lives at Prego. So does excellent nouvelle
★ Italian cuisine. The clientele looks older, wealthy, and is outfit-
ted in the latest fashions. They sit on *faux* zebra-skin chairs or
black banquettes and watch the flames in the high-tech black
kitchen (if they aren't watching themselves in the mirror). Every dish is relatively light and absolutely fresh. The *Insalata
Caprese* ($4.50) is a simple, satisfying salad of tomatoes, basil,
olive oil, and bocconcini cheese (like smoked mozzarella). Between courses you are given a small serving of sorbet; if you're
lucky, it will be the tarragon sorbet with poppy seeds sprinkled
in it. The linguine with tuna, tomatoes, and capers ($5.95) is
warm, light, and redolent of summer, even on a winter night.
An excellent main dish is *medaglione di vitello ai pistacchi*
($14.95), veal with cream, pistachios, fresh fruits, and
Frangelico (hazelnut liqueur). Keep some room for dessert, because Prego serves one that should be in a hall of fame
somewhere: *taramisu* ($5.95), a light cake with a filling of
sweet, creamy mascarpone cheese and a chocolate icing dusted
with cocoa. On the serving plate it sits next to a pool of sweet
vanilla and chocolate *crème* in a sunburst design crowned with
a single candied violet. It's a feast for the eyes and the mouth.
For such quality food, the prices are low. The service and wine
list are first rate. *5142 St. Lawrence Blvd., 5 blocks from Metro
Laurier, tel. 514/271–3234. Dress: informal but chic. Reservations a must. AE, CB, DC, MC, V.*

Moderate–Expensive **Bocca d'Oro.** This four-year-old Italian restaurant next to
Metro Guy has a huge menu offering a wide variety of appetiz-
ers, pastas, and veal and vegetarian dishes. One pasta specialty
is *tritico di pasta* ($11.95), which is one helping each of spinach
ravioli with salmon and caviar, shells marinara, and spaghetti
primavera. A good choice from the dozen or so veal dishes is
scallopine zingara ($16.50) with tomatoes, mushrooms, pick-
les, and olives. With the dessert and coffee the waiters bring
out a big bowl of walnuts for you to crack at your table (nut-
crackers provided). The two floors of dining rooms are
decorated with brass rails, wood paneling, and paintings, and
Italian pop songs play in the background. The staff is extremely friendly and professional; if you're in a hurry, they'll serve
your meal in record time. *1448 St. Mathieu St., downtown, tel.
514/933–8414. Dress: informal but neat. Reservations suggested. AE, CB, DC, MC, V. Closed Sun.*

Inexpensive **Pizza Pino.** This new, upscale pizza parlor is something of a dec-
orator's nightmare. The tablecloths are denim, large uncut cow
hides are draped on the walls, and the bar is burnished stain-
less steel. Triangle, circle, and square motifs are scattered
throughout. Behind the bar is an oven where are produced 24
kinds of pizza, from tomato and cheese ($4.25) to tomato, ham,
garlic, green pepper, and onions ($8.95). Despite the attention
spent on the decor, the kitchen knows its pizza; the crust is
good, and the toppings blend well together. Calzone and spaghetti are also available. For dessert, those with a sweet tooth
can try the various ice cream and pastry concoctions ($2.25–
$4.25). There's a short, uninteresting wine list, six beers on tap
and 18 in the bottle. The crowd is mostly students from
Concordia next door or McGill. *1471 Crescent St., downtown,*

tel. 514/844–4477. Dress: informal. Reservations rarely needed. AE, DC, MC, V.

Japanese

**Expensive–
Very Expensive**

Katsura. This cool, elegant Japanese restaurant introduced sushi (Japanese raw fish) to Montreal and is the haunt of business people who equate raw food with power. If you're with a group or just want privacy, you can reserve a tatami room closed off from the rest of the restaurant by rice-paper screens. Tatami are the straw mats you sit on (sans shoes) for a traditional Japanese dining experience. The sushi chefs create an assortment of raw seafood delicacies, as well as their own delicious invention, the Canada roll (smoked salmon and salmon caviar) at the sushi bar at the rear. Sushi connoisseurs may find some offerings less than top quality. The California rolls, for instance, are prepared in advance and refrigerated for a little too long. Katsura also serves some non-sushi dishes, like *Shabu-shabu*, a boiling hot-pot of broth in which thin slices of beef and vegetables are dipped ($34 for two). Teriyaki ($15.75) and tempura ($14.75) dishes tempt the less adventuresome. Katsura offers wine, sake, Japanese beer, and a number of house cocktails. The service is excellent, but if you sample all the sushi, the tab can be exorbitant. *2170 Mountain St., downtown between Metros Peel and Guy, tel. 514/849–1172. Dress: informal but neat. Reservations necessary, but you might get a seat at the sushi bar without them. AE, CB, DC, MC, V. No lunch weekends.*

Moroccan

**Moderate–
Expensive**

La Medina. Request a table at the back, where you sit under a Moroccan tent on low banquettes strewn with pillows for reclining. For those new to North African cuisine, the waiter usually recommends couscous royal ($15). The first course consists of four salads: eggplant, carrot, cucumbers with thyme, and green peppers with tomatoes. Then comes a mound of couscous (steamed semolina) with lamb and beef shish kebab piled around it. The suggested accompaniment is *boulaouane*, a tart yet refreshing "gray" wine halfway between rosé and white. During dinner there's a performance by a rather frenetic belly dancer; it's spectacular but not conducive to good digestion. The service can be slow, particularly when the waiter has his eye on the gyrating dancers. *3464 St. Denis St., tel. 514/282–0359. Dress: informal but neat. Reservations suggested. AE, CB, DC, MC, V.*

Quebecois

Expensive

Le Festin du Gouverneur. The Old Fort walls that enclose the David M. Stewart military museum also surround former stables that have been transformed into a 17th-century colonial banquet hall. Welcome to French-Canadian dinner-theater. For $30.80 per person you get a two-hour show, a four-course dinner, a cocktail, wine, and only one utensil: a knife. Everything is designed to re-create the days of New France 300 years ago. The dinner menu is liver pâté, creamy vegetable soup, beef brochette with quiche and vegetables, and apple pastry for dessert. Obviously, with only a knife, diners are forced to resort to their hands. (Bibs are available.) Entertainers in colonial dress provide period music, songs, and comedy sketches, all bilingual. The veneer of civilization seems to drop off when participants eat with their hands while fired by wine, and the banquets occasionally get loud and a bit bawdy. There are two sittings at 6 and 8:30 PM every day during the summer, while in the winter there's only a 7 PM show and that usually on Thursday, Friday, and Saturday. Le Festin du Gouverneur can be reached by car or via the Metro to the Île Ste-Hélène stop. The Old Fort is about a quarter-mile walk from the Metro station. Group rates are available. *St. Helen's Island, tel. 514/ 879–1141. Dress: informal. Reservations required. AE, CB, DC, MC, V.*

Moderate–Expensive ★ **Les Filles du Roy.** This restaurant serves fine Quebecois cuisine, a blend of 17th-century French recipes, North American produce and game, and some culinary tips picked up from Native Americans . . . with a lot of maple syrup poured over everything. The Trottier family opened Les Filles du Roy (the name refers to the women brought over to New France by Louis XIV to marry settlers) in an 18th-century stone mansion in 1964. If you want to go the native route—and you can eat excellent classic French cuisine as well—start with the "caribou" ($4.50), which is an eye-popping drink made of grain alcohol, sweet local wine, a dash of scotch, and Drambuie. The original recipe was concocted by hunters; it called for real caribou blood and homemade alcohol and provided warmth as well as vitamins. A traditional Quebecois meal starts with an appetizer like Canadian-style pork and beans or pea soup ($2.25). If you like sweet meat dishes, try the ham with maple syrup ($12.50). More refined dishes using local game and produce include wild lake duck with blueberries ($17) and *cipaille du Lac St. Jean*, which is a combination of six different meats, some wild, in a pie crust with vegetables. A large variety of maple syrup desserts are available: *trempette au sirop d'erable* ($3.75), pieces of bread that have been dipped in boiling maple syrup in a bowl of heavy cream; sugar pie ($2.75); and *oeuf cuit dans le sirop d'erable*, an egg poached in maple syrup. The popular Sunday brunch, served from 11 to 3, attracts groups of Japanese tourists wolfing down the ham and maple syrup dishes. The interior of Les Filles du Roy is all stone and wood, and the furniture looks authentic; the staff wears the usual colonial-era dress. The service is knowledgeable and friendly. *415 Bonsecours St., 3 blocks from Metro Champs de Mars in Old Montreal, tel. 514/ 849–3535. Dress: informal but neat. Reservations required. AE, DC, MC, V.*

Seafood

Very Expensive **Le Maritime.** Dover sole is the reason to visit this Ritz-Carlton restaurant. For $26 you can have it prepared one of 15 different ways, such as with almonds and butter; beer and endive; or mushrooms, white wine, and caviar. Unfortunately, the sole is usually frozen. The better varieties of sturgeon roe—imported from Petrossian in New York—are available at prices a little lower than Le Café de Paris upstairs. Excellent lobster, shrimp, and salmon dishes are also on the menu, as well as steak tartare ($18), veal, lamb, and chicken dishes for those who are dragged there by a fish fanatic. The potatoes and vegetables are often painstakingly sculpted into little flowers and other designs. The decor is low-key nautical with blue walls and maritime paintings. The waiters, as are all the Ritz's staff members, are consummate professionals. *1228 Sherbrooke St. W, tel. 514/842–4212. Jackets required. Reservations required. AE, DC, MC, V. Closed Sun.*

Expensive **Chez Delmo.** This stretch of Notre Dame Street is halfway be-
★ tween the courts and the stock exchange, and at lunchtime Chez Delmo is filled with professionals gobbling oysters and fish. The first room as you enter is lined with two long, dark, wood-and-brass bars, which are preferred by those wishing a fast lunch. Above both are murals depicting a medieval feast. The back room is a more sedate and cheerful dining room. One imagines that in the old days ladies were only allowed to sit back there only. In either room the dining is excellent and the seafood fresh. A good first course, or perhaps a light lunch, is the seafood salad ($8.95), a delicious mix of shrimp, lobster, crab, and artichoke hearts on a bed of Boston lettuce, sprinkled with a scalliony vinaigrette. The poached salmon with hollandaise ($15.75) is a nice slab of perfectly cooked fish with potatoes and broccoli. The lobsters and oysters are priced according to market rates. Chez Delmo was founded at the same address in 1910. The service is efficient and low-key. *211–215 Notre Dame St. W, Old Montreal, tel. 514/849–4061. Dress: informal but neat. Reservations suggested for dinner. AE, CB, DC, MC, V. No dinner Mon., no lunch Sat., closed Sun.*

8 Lodging

Introduction

On the island of Montreal alone there are more than 15,000 rooms available in every type of accommodation, from world-class luxury hotel to youth hostel, from student dormitory to budget executive motel. Keep in mind that during peak season (May–August), it may be difficult to find a bed without reserving.

Connoisseurs of luxury hotels go to Montreal to enjoy the six-star service of two world-class properties: the Ritz-Carlton and the Four Seasons (Le Quatre Saisons). The former occupies a central place in Montreal culture because of its age, its historical importance, and its position as a meeting place for the nationally and internationally powerful. Its grande-dame status is a result of its top-notch service and renowned gourmet restaurants. The only competitor is the Four Seasons, which offers ultra modern facilities, impeccable service, and comparable cuisine. Of the less expensive (but still pricey), convention-oriented hotels, the Queen Elizabeth (La Reine Elizabeth) and the Bonaventure Hilton International both stand out for having more individuality and less utilitarian corporate style than others in their class. Some may find the Hôtel de la Montagne overdecorated, but it is relatively inexpensive and features one of the city's top restaurants, Lutetia. In the moderate price range, the elegant and friendly Château Versailles is a gem. There are many small, cheap hotels on St. Hubert Street in both directions from the Voyageur bus station. Don't forget the hundreds of homes that provide inexpensive beds and breakfasts. The youth hostel, of course, has the cheapest bed in town.

Peak tourist season runs from May 1 to October 31, when many, but not all, hotels raise their prices. Thus prices often drop from November through April. Throughout the year a number of the better hotels have two-night, three-day, double occupancy packages that offer substantial discounts. During the off-season some hotels offer the "Montreal–50 Package," a 50% discount on all rooms from Thursday to Sunday inclusive. Montreal Tourism offices can provide details on both of these hotel packages. If the hotel you're interested in does not have either plan, it may have its own weekend or special package.

If you arrive in Montreal without a hotel reservation, the tourism information booths at either airport can provide you with a list of hotels and room availability. You must, however, make the reservation yourself. There are no information booths at the Voyageur bus terminal, but the Central Station is directly behind Queen Elizabeth Hotel and a block from the Quebec Tourism Center at Place Ville Marie.

The following list is comprised of recommended lodgings in Montreal for various budgets. Almost all of them are in the downtown area. There are no hotels in Old Montreal, although you will find some bed and breakfasts there.

The rates quoted are for a standard double room in August 1988; off-season rates are almost always lower. The following credit card abbreviations are used: AE, American Express; CB, Carte Blanche; DC, Diners Club; MC, MasterCard; V, Visa.

Montreal Lodging

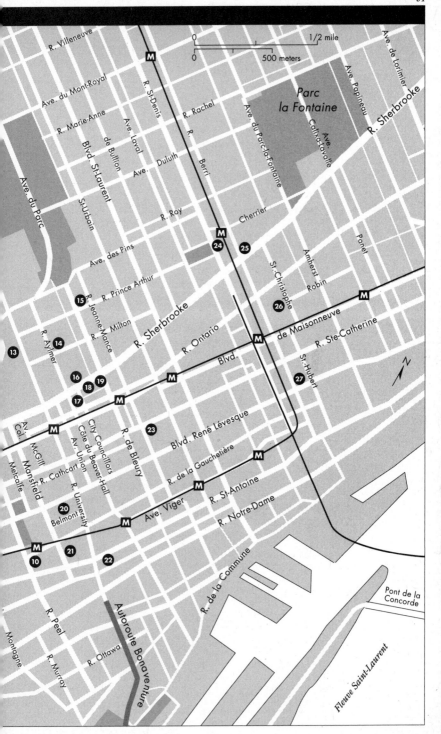

Highly recommended hotels in each price category are indicated by a star ★.

Category	Cost*
Very Expensive	over $150
Expensive	$95–$150
Moderate	$50–$95
Inexpensive	under $50

All prices are for a standard double room, excluding an optional service charge.

Downtown

Very Expensive
★

Bonaventure Hilton International. This 400-room Hilton, situated atop a Metro station, the Place Bonaventure exhibition center, and a mall crowded with shops and restaurants, is, first and foremost, a resort hotel—17 floors above the street. When you exit the elevator at 17, you find yourself in a spacious reception area flanked by an outdoor swimming pool (heated year-round) and 2½ acres of gardens, complete with ducks. Also on this floor is a complex of three restaurants and a nightclub that features well-known international entertainers. Le Castillon is the flagship restaurant, known for its three-course, 55-minute businessman's lunch and high quality cuisine (*see* Dining). On Sunday, Gypsy night, the fare is Russian. All rooms have fully stocked mini-bars and black-and-white TV in the bathroom. The Bonaventure has excellent access to the Metro station of the same name beneath it and to all the shops at Place Ville Marie through the Underground City. *1 Place Bonaventure, tel. 514/878-2332 or 800/445-8667. 400 rooms. Facilities: 3 restaurants, nightclub, health club with sauna, outdoor pool, rooftop garden, gift shop (hotel is located in a building with a shopping mall), 24-hr room service. AE, CB, DC, MC, V.*

Le Château Champlain. In the heart of downtown Montreal, at the southern end of Place du Canada, the Château Champlain is a 36-floor skyscraper with distinctive half-moon-shaped windows. The decor of this Canadian Pacific hotel is glitzy-modern and the scale is big; the hotel specializes in the convention crowd. Five restaurants offer different ways of entertaining expense-account clients, from formal gourmandizing or tropical-style dining and dancing to high-stepping can-can girls. You can work off the excesses of appetite at Le Spa, a health club with an exercise room, saunas, and a large indoor pool. Two floors are reserved for nonsmokers. Underground passageways connect the Champlain with the Bonaventure Metro station, the Bonaventure Hilton International, and Place Ville Marie. *1 Place du Canada, tel. 514/878-9000 or 800/828-7447. 614 rooms. Facilities: 3 restaurants, lounge with entertainment, health club with sauna and whirlpool, large indoor pool, movie theater, gift shops. AE, CB, DC, MC, V.*

Le Meridien. This Air France property rises from the center of the Complexe Desjardins, a boutique-rich mall in the center of the plushest stretch of the Underground City. The Place des Arts and the Metro stop of the same name are mere meters in one direction, the Complexe Guy-Favreau mall and the convention center the same distance in the other. The hotel caters to businesspeople and tourists who want ultramodern European style and convenience. The Meridien is designed on a plan of circles of privilege within these already-exclusive surroundings. For instance, within Le Café Fleuri French restaurant there's a chicer, pricier enclave called Le Club. The ninth floor of the hotel, Le Club President, is reserved for businesspeople who demand *ne plus ultra* service. Toiletries are by Hèrmes throughout. There's also a no-smoking floor and an indoor pool, sauna, and whirlpool facility. And if the atmosphere ever seems too confining, you can always burst out the door and go to Chinatown, a block away. *4 Complexe Desjardins, tel. 514/285–1450 or 800/543–4300. 601 rooms. Facilities: 3 restaurants, piano bar, indoor pool, sauna, whirlpool, sauna, guest passes to nearby YMCA and YWCA, babysitting services; located in complex with shops and boutiques. AE, CB, DC, MC, V.*

★ **The Four Seasons (Le Quartre Saisons).** The "Golden Square Mile" of Sherbrooke Street West—Montreal's Fifth Avenue—is decorated by the city's two best hotels. The Ritz-Carlton and this property are engaged in a constant battle to see which can give its clients the best and most in services. Even the least expensive room, known as a "Superior," has amenities galore: three phones, bathrobes, silk hangers, a minibar, a hair dryer, a clock-radio, and a safe. The more expensive suites have even more phones, and some are graced with marble bathtubs like the one Michael Jackson presumably floated in when he was a guest. The Four Seasons is renovated frequently, and the latest decor is at the same time slickly modern and filled with "stately English manor" furnishings. The white-columned Le Restaurant is known as one of Montreal's best places for nouvelle cuisine *(see* Dining). The other two eateries are more informal. The Gym Tech Fitness center, filled with strange-looking machines, is available for guests' use for a fee, and there's also a heated, year-round, outdoor pool. The Four Seasons is one block from Metro Peel in the heart of Montreal's fanciest shopping district. *1050 Sherbrooke St. W, tel. 514/284–1110 or 800/332–3442. 300 rooms. Facilities: 3 restaurants, lounge, health club with whirlpool and sauna, outdoor pool, 24-hr room service. AE, CB, DC, MC, V.*

★ **Ritz-Carlton.** This property floats like a stately old luxury liner along Sherbrooke Street. It was opened in 1912 by a consortium of local investors who wanted a hotel in which their rich European friends could stay and indulge their champagne and caviar tastes. Since then many earth-shaking events have occurred here, including one of the marriages of Elizabeth Taylor and Richard Burton. Power breakfasts, lunches, and dinners are the rule at the elegant Café de Paris, and the Prime Minister and others in the national government are frequently sighted eating here. A less heady atmosphere prevails at the Ritz-Carlton's three other excellent restaurants. Guest rooms are a successful blend of Edwardian style—working fireplaces—with such modern accessories as electronic safes. Careful and personal attention are hallmarks of the Ritz-Carlton's service. The clientele is corporate rather than conventioneer, luxury-loving rather than packaged. There is no health club or a swimming pool on the premises; the Ritz-Carlton remains true to another tradition, that of hiring others to do your physical labor. *1228 Sherbrooke St. W, tel. 514/842–4212 or 800/223–9868. 240 rooms. Facilities: 4 restaurants, piano bar, Holt Renfrew department store, beauty salon, barber shop, 24-hr room service. AE, CB, DC, MC, V.*

Expensive **Delta Montreal.** Spanking new and French-styled, the Delta is
making a bid to break into the ranks of Montreal's world-class
hotels. Many of the spacious guest rooms have balconies and excellent views of the city. The Le Bouquet restaurant and the
piano lounge are designed like 19th-century Parisian establishments with dark wood panelling and brass chandeliers. The
cuisine is Continental and not above trendy touches like grill-
ing over mesquite. The Delta has the most complete exercise
and pool facility in Montreal. There are indoor and outdoor
pools, two international squash courts, an exercise room, a sauna, and a whirlpool. The innovative Children's Creative Centre
lets your children play (under supervision) while you gallivant
around town. *450 Sherbrooke St. W (entrance off President-
Kennedy), tel. 514/286–1986 or 800/268–1133. 458 rooms. Facilities: restaurant; jazz bar (which also serves lunch Mon.–
Fri.); indoor and outdoor pools; health club with whirlpool,
sauna, squash courts, aerobic classes; children's center; gift
shop. AE, CB, DC, MC, V.*

La Citadelle. There's a small pack of hotels on Sherbrooke
Street, all of them convenient to Place des Arts, shopping, and
the financial district; the Citadelle, a Quality Inn property, is
one of them. This relatively small business hotel offers low-key
atmosphere and service, along with all the features of its
better-known brethren: minibars, in-room movies, a small
health club with an indoor pool, etc. There's also a passable
French restaurant, Le Châtelet. *410 Sherbrooke St. W, tel. 514/
844–8851 or 800/361–7545. 180 rooms. Facilities: restaurant,
lounge with entertainment, health club with sauna and steam
room, indoor pool, gift shop. AE, DC, MC, V.*

Le Centre Sheraton. In a huge 37-story complex well placed between the downtown business district and the restaurant
streets of Crescent and Bishop, this Sheraton offers a wide variety of services to both the business and tourist crowds. There
are three restaurants, five lounges; a nightclub, indoor pool,
and health club; plus indoor parking for 600 cars. The elite,
five-story Towers section is geared toward business travelers.
The Sheraton caters to conventions, so expect to encounter
such groups when you stay here. Though the decor is beige and
unremarkable (once inside you could be inside any large, modern hotel in any North American metropolis), the location's the
thing. *1201 René Lévesque Blvd. W, tel. 514/878–2000 or 800/
325–3535. 824 rooms. Facilities: 3 restaurants, 5 lounges,
nightclub, health club with whirlpool and sauna, indoor pool,
unisex beauty parlor, gift shop. AE, CB, DC, MC, V.*

Moderate **Le Baccarat Comfort Inn.** Completely renovated in 1988, this
medium-size, medium-price hotel, next to the McGill campus,
caters to the business trade. A small pool and health club were
added and the lobby was redone. The decor of the restaurant is
metallic, disco-style, and the cuisine is not recommendable. Le
Baccarat is handy to downtown business and shopping areas.
*475 Sherbrooke St. W, tel. 514/842–3961 or 800/228–5150. 200
rooms. Facilities: restaurant, cafe, piano bar, health club, indoor pool (not in service as of this writing). AE, CB, DC, MC,
V.*

★ **Le Grand Hôtel.** The Grand Hotel abuts the stock exchange;
Place Bonaventure is half a block one way, the western fringe
of Old Montreal one block the other, and the Metro Square Victoria can be reached via underground passage. In the midst of
all this, The Grand Hotel rises above a stunning three-story

atrium-reception area. It's yet another large, modern hotel attractive to meeting planners. With the same owners as the Copley Plaza in Boston, the Grand Hotel offers the usual health club and pool facilities, a more exclusive floor for higher-paying guests, and a shopping arcade on the underground level. Its most outstanding feature: the restaurants. The Tour de Ville on the top floor is the city's only revolving restaurant, and its bar has live jazz nightly. The newly renovated Chez Antoine is an Art Nouveau-style bistro with grilled meats a specialty (*see* Dining). *777 University St., tel. 514/879–1370 or 800/361–8155. 737 rooms. Facilities: 2 restaurants, bar, health club with spa and steam room, aerobic classes, indoor pool, gift shop. AE, DC, MC, V.*

Holiday Inn Crowne Plaza. The flagship of the Holiday Inn chain's downtown Montreal hotels, the Crowne Plaza could just as well have been plopped down in Las Vegas or Atlanta. On the other hand, one doesn't stay in Holiday Inns for originality of design. This hotel *does* sparkle: It was just renovated from top to bottom. Indoor pool, health club, café-restaurant, two bars: it's all here. Popular for conventions, this hotel is near Metro Place des Arts, Sherbrooke Street shopping, downtown. *420 Sherbrooke St. W, tel. 514/842–6111 or 800/465–4329. 487 rooms. Facilities: café-restaurant, 2 bars, indoor pool, health club with sauna and whirlpool, unisex beauty parlor, gift shop. AE, DC, MC, V.*

Holiday Inn Richelieu. Chocolate brown is the predominant color in the Richelieu. This hotel is near Metro Sherbrooke, the Square St. Louis, the restaurants of St. Denis Street, and the summertime nightlife of Prince Arthur Street. The Richelieu has an indoor pool, a restaurant, and a bar. Its good location makes you want to spend a lot of time outdoors. *505 Sherbrooke St. E, tel. 514/842–8581 or 800/465–4329. 330 rooms. Facilities: restaurant, bar, indoor pool, sauna, gift shop. AE, CB, DC, MC, V.*

★ **Hôtel de la Montagne.** The reception area of the Hôtel de la Montagne greets you with a naked, butterfly-winged nymph rising out of a fountain. An enormous crystal chandelier hangs from the ceiling and tinkles to the beat of disco music played a little too loudly. The decor says Versailles rebuilt with a dash of Art Nouveau by a discotheque architect circa 1975. Some puritanical tastes might find it overdone ("Naked nymphs!"), but others will find it fun. The rooms are tamer but large and comfortable. Another excellent reason to stay in or visit this hotel is the food. The main restaurant, La Lutetia, is known as one of the best and most innovative gourmet eateries in Montreal. There are three other restaurants offering less expensive, faster meals and an extremely popular dance club called Thursday's. Most of the guests are French-speaking, and the restaurants and Thursday's attract a big local crowd. If you're staying elsewhere the reception area is at least worth a visit. *1430 Mountain St. tel. 514/288–5656 or 800/361–6262. 132 rooms. Facilities: 2 restaurants, disco-bar, outdoor pool. AE, DC, MC, V.*

Hôtel Maritime. This medium-size hotel next to the Grey Nun's Museum and Convent on René Lévesque Boulevard was recently overhauled. The decor is now somewhat spartan and ultramodern, with recessed colored lights casting pastel glows around the mirrored reception area. There's an indoor pool and a circular French restaurant, Le Beau Rivage, with a mediocre reputation. The rooms are painted from a palette of cream, peach, and pale caramel. The Maritime's clientele is generally French-speaking. *1155 Guy St. (2 blocks from Metro Guy), tel. 514/932–1411 or 800/363–6255. 215 rooms. Facilities: restaurant, piano bar, indoor pool. AE, CB, DC, MC, V.*

Ramada Renaissance du Parc. The Ramada chain bought the old Hôtel du Parc in July 1987 and has made it the most luxurious of its four Montreal properties. Half a block away from the acres of greenery in Mount Royal Park, this Ramada's locale is prime. The hotel itself aims its services mainly at a corporate clientele. The rooms are large, and the decor is modern and well maintained. Health-minded guests may use the adjoining Club La Cité, which has squash and tennis courts, whirlpools and saunas, weight room, exercise classes, and an indoor-outdoor pool. From the lobby you can descend to a shopping mall with many stores and a movie theater. The nightlife of Prince Arthur Street is six blocks away. *3625 Park Ave., tel. 514/288–6666 or 800/228–9898. 456 rooms. Facilities: restaurant, café-bar, lounge, health club with sauna, whirlpool, squash and tennis courts, indoor-outdoor pool, 24-hr room service, gift shop. AE, CB, DC, MC, V.*

★ **Queen Elizabeth.** If the Ritz-Carlton is a stately old cruise ship, then the Queen Elizabeth, also called La Reine Elizabeth, is a battleship. Massive and gray, this hotel sits on top of the Central Train Station in the very heart of the city, across the street from the Catholic Cathedral and Place Ville Marie. The lobby is a bit too much like a railway station—hordes march this way and that—to be attractive and personal, but upstairs the rooms are modern, spacious, and spotless, especially in the more expensive Entrée Gold section. All the latest gadgets and other trappings of luxury are present. The Beaver Club (*see* Dining), the flagship restaurant, is such an institution that there is a small museum devoted to it on the lobby level. There's a cheaper restaurant, too, as well as Arthur's supper club, and four lounges. Conventions are a specialty here. *900 René Lévesque Blvd. W, tel. 514/861–3511 or 800/268–9143. 1,045 rooms. Facilities: 2 restaurants, supper club, 4 bars/lounges, gift shops. AE, CB, DC, MC, V.*

Le Shangrila. If you're a frequent traveler to Montreal, you may want to try something different: an Oriental-style hotel. Le Shangrila is situated across the street from the Four Seasons on Sherbrooke Street, one block from Metro Peel. Owned by a businesswoman from Singapore of Chinese descent, the hotel's decor from reception to restaurant to rooms is modern with an amalgam of Korean, Chinese, Japanese, and Indian motifs and artwork. The management claims that its rooms are among the largest in square footage in downtown Montreal. A large Szechuan-style restaurant Dynastie de Ming opened on the lobby level in mid-1988. The Shangrila has no health club or pool; for these you'll have to go across the street to the Four Seasons and pay. During the week the clientele is corporate, while on weekends most of the guests are tourists from the United States and Ontario. *3407 Peel St., tel. 514/288–4141 or 800/361–7791. 166 rooms. Facilities: restaurant, bar. AE, CB, DC, MC, V.*

★ **Château Versailles.** This small, charming hotel occupies a row of four converted mansions in an excellent location on Sherbrooke Street West. The owners have decorated it with many antique paintings, tapestries, and furnishings; some rooms have ornate moldings and plaster decorations on the walls and ceilings. Each room also has a full bath, TV, and air-conditioning. The reception area is designed to look like a European pension. There's no restaurant at the Versailles, though breakfast is served in the Breakfast Room, and afternoon tea is available from room service. The staff is extremely helpful and friendly. The Versailles is unassuming, not too expensive, and classy. *1659 Sherbrooke St. W (near Metro Guy), tel. 514/933–3611 or 800/361–3664. 70 rooms. Facilities: breakfast room; room service offers tea and biscuits in the evening. AE, MC, V.*

Hôtel de l'Institut. The Quebec Institute of Tourism and Hôtellerie, an official government agency, owns and operates the Hôtel de l'Institut, a training academy for future hotel and restaurant managers. The exterior looks like a prefab office building constructed by the phone company; the interior is more attractive, although still a bit institutional. The service, however, is excellent (after all, they're getting graded on it). The rooms are small and comfortable, but a bit outmoded. Both the hotel and the restaurant are good values, and reservations may be difficult to get. Hôtel de l'Institut is on top of the Metro Sherbrooke station and near the Prince Arthur Street pedestrian mall. *3535 St. Denis St., tel. 514/282–5120. 42 rooms. Facilities: restaurant, free Continental breakfast, bar. AE, CB, DC, MC, V.*

Lord Berri. Next to the University of Quebec–Montreal, the Lord Berri is a new, moderately priced hotel convenient to the restaurants and nightlife of St. Denis Street. It offers some of the services of its more expensive competition: minibars, in-room movies, and nonsmoking floors. The De La Muse restaurant serves good bistro food and is popular with a local clientele. The Berri–UQAM Metro stop is a block away. *1199 Berri St., tel. 514/845–9236 or 800/363–0363. 154 rooms. Facilities: restaurant, gift shop. AE, DC, MC, V.*

Le Nouvel Hôtel. The Nouvel Hôtel is what hotel managers like to call a "new concept"—it offers a little of everything: studios, suites, 2½ to 4½-room apartments. It's not very classy, but it's all new, bright-colored, and functionable. Some time in 1988 management plans to open a health club and an indoor pool. The Nouvel Hôtel is near the restaurant district, five or six blocks from the heart of downtown, and two blocks from the Guy Metro station. *1740 René Lévesque Blvd. W, tel. 514/931–8841 or 800/567–2737. 481 rooms. Facilities: restaurant, supper club with entertainment, free Continental breakfast, gift shop, full health club, and indoor pool (under construction.) AE, DC, MC, V.*

Roussillon Royal. This hotel is adjacent to the Terminus Voyageur bus station (buses park directly beneath one wing of the hotel) and some of the bus station aura seems to rub off on the Roussillon; it's a little dingy. But if you're stumbling off of a long bus ride and want somewhere to stay, *now*, the Roussillon's rooms are large and clean, the service is friendly, and the price is right. It's also handy to the Berri–UQAM Metro station. *1610 St. Hubert St., tel. 514/849–3214. 104 rooms. Facilities: restaurant under construction (late 1988). AE, DC, MC, V.*

Inexpensive **YMCA.** This clean, modern Y is downtown, next to Peel Metro station. *1450 Stanley St., tel. 514/849–8393. 352 rooms. MC, V.*

YWCA. Very close to dozens of restaurants the Y is three blocks from downtown. *1355 René Lévesque Blvd. W, tel. 514/866–9941. 117 rooms. MC, V.*

McGill University Area

Inexpensive **Auberge de Jeunesse International de Montreal.** The youth hostel near the McGill campus in the student ghetto charges $12 a night per person. Reserve early during the summer tourist season. *3541 Aylmer St., tel. 514/843–3317. 108 beds. Facilities: Rooms for four to 12 people (same sex); a few rooms available for couples and families. No credit cards.*

McGill Student Apartments. From mid-May to mid-August, when McGill is on summer recess, you can stay in its dorms on the grassy, quiet campus in the heart of the city. *3935 University St., tel. 514/398–6367. 1,000 rooms. Facilities: campus swimming pool and health facilities (visitors must pay to use them). No credit cards.*

University of Montreal Area

Inexpensive **University of Montreal Residence.** The university's student housing accepts visitors from May 9 to August 22. It's on the other side of Mount Royal, a long walk from downtown and Old Montreal, but there's the new University of Montreal Metro stop right next to the campus. *2350 Edouard Montpetit Blvd., tel. 514/343–6531. 1,171 rooms. Facilities: campus sports center with pool and gym (visitors must pay to use it). No credit cards.*

Bed-and-Breakfasts

Downtown B & B Network. This organization will put you in touch with 75 homes and apartments, mostly around the downtown core and along Sherbrooke Street, that have one or more rooms available for visitors. These homes generally are clean, lovingly kept-up, and filled with antiques. The hosts generously dole out, with breakfast, recommendations about what to see and do during your day in Montreal. Even during the height of the tourist season, this organization has rooms open. *Contact: Bob Finkelstein, 3458 Laval St. (at Sherbrooke St.), Montreal H2X 3C8, tel. 514/289–9749. Single $25–$40, double $35–$50. AE, MC, V.*

Montreal Bed and Breakfast. Founded in 1979, this is the oldest B & B agency in Montreal. Most of the more than 50 homes are in the elegant English neighborhood of Westmount, in Outremont, or downtown. Some of them can be quite ritzy, like the entire floor of a centuries-old stone house in Old Montreal ($100 a night). Others are less expensive, but all provide breakfast and a wealth of information about the city. Visitors who take a Gray Line tour get a 15% discount on the cost of one night's lodging. *Contact: Marian Kahn, 4912 Victoria, Montreal H3W 2N1, tel. 514/738–9410. Single $30–$50, double $45–$100. The deposit may be made with American Express, MasterCard, or Visa, but the balance must be paid with cash or traveler's checks.*

9 The Arts and Nightlife

When it comes to entertainment, Montreal has a superiority complex. It can boast of serious culture—symphony orchestras, opera and dance companies. At the pinnacle of the High Art scene stands the Montreal Symphony Orchestra, led by Charles Dutoit, and the Opera of Montreal. The city is known for its adventurous theatrical companies; unfortunately for the English-speaking visitor, most presentations are in French. Montreal is also the home of a small group of filmmakers who regularly bring home accolades from international festivals. On the low-life side of the tracks, the city is filled with all types of bars and clubs, including jazz and rock clubs, discos, cabarets, singles bars, and strip clubs. Puritanism is definitely not in fashion here. There are also a number of larger halls where international pop and rock stars regularly perform. Summer is the time for the most action—more events, bigger crowds, later hours—but if you visit during the off-season there's sure to be something going on.

The entertainment section of the *Gazette*, the English-language daily paper, is a good place to scope out upcoming events. The Friday weekend guide has an especially good list of all events at the city's concert halls, theaters, clubs, dance spaces, and movie houses. The "Best Bets" column goes beyond the listings to descriptions of the most interesting shows. *Montreal Scope*, a free monthly magazine available in many hotels, points you to the strictly "tourist" entertainment, shopping, and restaurants. The city cultural authorities distribute a free brochure to concerts and other events in the Place des Arts complex. The brochure is available at tourist information centers and at the larger hotels.

For tickets to major pop and rock concerts, shows, festivals, and hockey, baseball, and football games, go to the individual box offices or call **Ticketron** (tel. 514/288–3651). Ticketron outlets are located in La Baie department store, in all Sears stores, and downtown at Square Philips. Place des Arts tickets may be purchased at its box office underneath the Salle Wilfrid Pelletier, next to the Metro station. **Les Enterprises Dupont et Dupont** (tel. 514/843–3177) sells restaurant-theater ticket packages that get you a reservation at a restaurant near the theater and a good seat for the show.

The Arts

Music

The **Montreal Symphony Orchestra** has gained world renown under the baton of Charles Dutoit. When not on tour its regular venue is the Salle Wilfrid Pelletier at the Place des Arts. The orchestra also gives Christmas and summer concerts in the Notre-Dame Basilica and pops concerts at the Arena Maurice Richard in the Olympic Park. For information, call 514/842–3402. McGill University (tel. 514/487–5190) is also the site of many classical concerts, the most notable given by the **McGill Chamber Orchestra.** The **Opera of Montreal,** founded in 1980, stages five productions a year at Place des Arts (tel. 514/521–5577).

The 20,000-seat **Montreal Forum** (tel. 514/932–6131) and the much larger Olympic Stadium are where rock and pop concerts are staged. More intimate concert halls include the **Théâtre St. Denis** (1594 St. Denis St., tel. 514/849–4211) and the **Spectrum** (318 St. Catherine St. W, tel. 514/861–5851).

Theater

French-speaking theater lovers will find a wealth of dramatic productions. There are at least 10 major companies in town, some of which have an international reputation. (See sources above for current productions.) Anglophones have less to choose from, unless they want to chance the language barrier. **Centaur Theatre,** the best-known English theatrical company, stages productions in the Beaux-Arts–style former stock exchange building at 453 St. Francis-Xavier Street in Old Montreal (tel. 514/288–3161). English-language plays can also be seen at the **Saidye Bronfman Center** at 5170 Côte St. Catherine. Michel Tremblay is Montreal's premier playwright, and any of his plays are worth seeing, even if in the English translation. Touring companies of Broadway productions can often be seen at the **Théâtre St. Denis** on St. Denis Street (tel. 514/849–4211).

Dance

Traditional and contemporary dance companies thrive in Montreal, though many take to the road or are on hiatus in the summer. The best-known, **Les Grands Ballets Canadiens,** performs at Place des Arts when not on tour. In September, the **Festival International de Nouvelle Danse** brings "new dance" to various venues around town. And **Tangente** (tel. 514/842–3532) at 3655 St. Lawrence Street, is the home of the more avantgarde dance troupes.

Film

While not quite Hollywood, Montreal is the site of five major film festivals—the **Montreal World Film Festival** in late August is the most notable—and thus the heart of Canada's film industry. Many U.S. producers like to film here because costs are lower. Local filmmakers frequently garner praise at international competitions and, of course, have an avid following. There are well over 75 first-run movie houses in town—see the *Gazette* for listings—with films in both French and English. Read the ads carefully or you may find yourself watching a recent Hollywood release, like *Wall Street,* dubbed in French. There are also many revival cinemas in Montreal, a sample of which includes **Cinémathèque Québécoise** (335 de Maisonneuve Boulevard, tel. 514/842–9768), **Ouimetoscope** (1204 St. Catherine St. E, tel. 514/525–8600), **Cinéma de Paris** (896 St. Catherine St. W, tel. 514/866–3636), and **Cinéma V** (5560 Sherbrooke St. W, tel. 514/489– 5559).

Nightlife

Bars and Clubs

Small, cabaret-type shows can be found at a few major hotels. **Arthur's Café Baroque** at the Queen Elizabeth (tel. 514/861–

3511) stages can-can/Charleston revue that rates a PG; **Le Café Conc** at the Château Champlain (tel. 514/878–9000) is a bit more risque. (For fleshier extravaganzas, try the strip clubs along St. Catherine St. downtown.) The **Music Hall** in Le Nouvel Hotel (tel. 514/931–8841) has comic dinner shows. **Le Portage** at the Bonaventure Hilton International (tel. 514/878–2323) presents popular performances, like Ben E. King and the Mamas and the Papas. There is music and slow dancing at **Puzzle's Jazz Bar** in the Ramada Renaissance (tel. 514/288-3733), the Sheraton's **L'Impromptu** (tel. 514/878–2000), and the **Tour de Ville,** atop the Grand Hotel (tel. 514/879-1370).

Jazz Montreal has a very active local jazz scene. The best-known club is Old Montreal's **L'Air du Temps** (191 St. Paul St. W, tel. 514/842–2003). This small, smokey club presents 90% local talent and 10% international acts from 5 PM on into the night. There's a cover charge Thursday through Saturday. If you like jazz and you're downtown, duck into **Biddle's** (tel. 514/842-8656) at 2060 Aylmer Street, where bassist Charles Biddle holds forth most evenings when he's not appearing at a local hotel. This upscale club is also a restaurant that serves ribs and chicken, so lick the bones clean and start drumming. Cover charge for the big acts. You also might try **Club Jazz 2080** (tel. 514/285–0007) at 2080 Clark Street or **Le Grand Café** (tel. 514/849–6955) at 1720 St. Denis Street.

Rock Rock clubs seem to spring up, flourish, then fizzle out overnight. **Club Soda** (tel. 514/270–7848) at 5240 Park Avenue, the granddaddy of them all, sports a neon martini glass complete with neon effervescence outside. Inside it's a small hall with a stage, three bars, and rooms for about 400 people. International rock acts play here as well as local talent. It's also a venue for the comedy and jazz festivals. Open seven nights from 8 PM to 3 AM; admission ranges from nothing up to $20, depending. **Foufounes Électriques** (tel. 514/845–5484)—which translates as "electric buns"—at 97 St. Catherine Street East in the Latin Quarter, is the downscale, more avant-garde competitor to Club Soda. Foufounes is the center for the local band scene and also attracts up-and-coming acts from the United States. There's a "quiet" section for conversation and a "loud" section for music and dancing. Open daily from 3 PM to 3 AM, admission variable. Other clubs include **Déjà Vu** (1224 Bishop St., tel. 514/866–0512), **Station 10** (2071 St. Catherine St. W, tel. 514/934-0484), **Secrets** (40 Pine Ave. W, tel. 514/844–0004) and **Night Magic** (22 St. Paul St. E, tel. 514/861–8143) in Old Montreal.

Discos

Montrealers are as into discos as you could imagine. The newest and the glitziest is **Metropolis** (tel. 514/288–5559) at 59 St. Catherine Street East. The crowd is young, French, and clad in black. This club is reminiscent of New York's Palladium in that the enormous space (a former theater where Sarah Bernhardt performed) has been given a complete workover by local architects, and it has high-powered light and sound systems. It's open Thursday through Sunday, and the admission is $5 unless a band is appearing. Many of the hotels have discos, and they're scattered throughout the nightlife areas around Crescent and St. Denis streets. The more popular ones are **Thunder Dome**

(1254 Stanley St., tel. 514/397–1628), **Le Business** (3500 St. Lawrence Blvd., tel. 514/844–3988), and the **Diamond Club** (1186 Crescent St., tel. 514/866–4048).

Singles Bars

Singles bars center around Crescent, Bishop, and Mountain streets. The two mainstays are **Thursday's**—the city's best-known—and the **Sir Winston Churchill Pub** at nos. 1449 and 1459 Crescent Street. Emulators of the former are **Thirsty's** (1187 Bishop St.) and **Friday's** (636 Cathcart St.). The athletic set unwinds at **La Cage aux Sports,** not too far from the Forum at 2250 Guy Street. Another bar scene takes place on Prince Arthur Street. The French-flavored **Vol de Nuit** at no. 14 is the *classiest* joint there. **Le Keg** (22 St. Paul St. E) is known as a place for raucous carousing in Old Montreal. A quieter, more sophisticated (and probably more expensive) evening can be had at one of the bars in the better hotels, the **Grand Prix Bar** in the Ritz-Carlton being the classiest.

10 Excursions

by Patricia Lowe

Montreal has two major attractions beyond its city limits: the Laurentian mountain range to the north and the Eastern Townships or Estrie between Montreal and the Vermont and New York borders. The Laurentians are characterized by thousands of miles of unspoiled wilderness and world-famous ski resorts. The Townships have rolling hills and farmland. As major vacation areas in both winter and summer, they offer outdoor activities on ski slopes and lakes, and in their provincial parks.

The Laurentians

Avid skiers might call Montreal a bedroom community for the Laurentians, just 35 miles (56 kilometers) to the north and home to some of North America's best-known ski resorts. The Laurentian range is ancient, dating to the Precambrian era (600,000 years ago). These rocky hills are relatively low, worn down by glacial activity, but they include eminently skiable hills, with a few peaks above 2,500 feet (760 meters). World-famous Mount Tremblant, at 3,150 feet (960 meters), is the tallest.

Getting Around

By Car Quebec Autoroute 15, a six-lane highway, and the slower but more scenic secondary road 117 lead to this resort country.

By Bus Frequent bus service is available from the Voyageur bus terminal on Berri Street in downtown Montreal, and in winter a special Aeroski bus service operates from both Dorval and Mirabel airports. The Quebec tourism office, has information on the Laurentians; while the Laurentian tourist association is manned by helpful experts at its office in St-Jérôme—the gateway to these mountains—off Autoroute Exit 39 on Route 15.

Outfitters

Outfitters recommended by the Laurentian tourist association include **Pourvoirie des 100 Lacs,** run by Claude Lavigne (tel. 514/659–4155); **Club de Chasse** and **Pêche du Lac Beauregard** in St-Jovite (tel. 819/425–7722); and **Club des Guides** at Lac-Du-Cerf, Raymond Webster (tel. 819/597–2011). Before setting off into the wilds, consult the Quebec Outfitters Association (514/687–0041) or ask for its list of outfitters available through tourist offices.

Exploring

With the advent of snow-making equipment the resorts of Les Laurentides, as they are called, are year-round attractions. A number of large hotels have added indoor pools and spa facilities, and efficient highways have brought the country closer to the city—45 minutes to St-Sauveur, 1½–2 hours to Mount Tremblant. Montrealers drive up to enjoy the fall foliage or engage in spring skiing and are home before dark. The only difficult periods are early October when there is nothing to do and June when there is plenty to do but also a lot of black flies.

The vacation area truly begins at St. Sauveur-des-Monts (Exit 60) and extends as far north as Mount Tremblant. Then it turns into a wilderness of lakes, some with private chalets and fishing camps, and forests best visited with an outfitter. Laurentian guides planning fishing and hunting trips are concentrated around St. Donat near Mount Tremblant Park.

Numbers in the margin correspond with points of interest on the Laurentians map.

To the first-time visitor, the hills and resorts around St-Sauveur, Ste-Marguerite Station, Morin Heights, Val Morin and Val David, up to Ste-Agathe, form a pleasant hodgepodge of villages, hotels, and inns that seem to blend one into another. Actually, **St-Sauveur-des-Monts** dominates a number of communities, like Piedmont, and is the center of Montreal's closest vacationland.

In the summer holiday-makers make for its golf courses (two of the more pleasant are 18-hole links at Ste-Adèle and Mont Gabriel), campgrounds at Val David, Lacs Claude, and Lafontaine and beaches; in the fall and winter, they come for foliage and alpine as well as nordic skiing.

An old favorite with Montrealers, the 300-room **Le Chantecler** on Lac Rond in Ste-Adèle, is nestled at the base of a mountain with 22 downhill ski runs. Skiing is the obvious draw—trails begin almost at the hotel entrance. Summer activities include tennis, golf, and boating. An indoor pool and spa, as well as a beach, make swimming a year-round possibility. There are a number of rate plans available, like a special summer package starting at $105 per day, but expect to pay between $240 and $309 double. *Box 1048, Ste-Adèle, tel. 514/229–3555.*

The busy town of **Ste-Adèle** is full of gift and Quebec craft shops, boutiques, and restaurants. It also has the most active nightlife in the Laurentians, including a few discos. A couple of miles north on Highway 117, the reconstructed **Village de Seraphin**'s 20 small habitant homes, grand country house, general store, and church recall the settlers who came to Ste-Adèle in the 1840s. The historic town also features a train tour through the woods. *Tel. 514/229–4777. Admission: $6 adults, $3 children 5–11. Open late May–early Oct.*

Ste-Marguerite Station is home to the large family-style **Alpine Inn,** a log cabin main house with separate chalets for rent. Surrounded by rolling ski hills and manicured grounds it features good dining, golf (CPGA pro for lessons), a putting green, swimming pools (indoor and out), and one of the Laurentians' most scenic cross-country ski trails.

The social director organizes folksy summer barbecues around the pool and there are two-night packages available. *Chemin Ste-Marguerite, tel. 514/229–3516 or 800/363–2577. Regular rates run from about $215 double to $382, Modified American Plan (MAP), two meals a day.*

At Autoroute exit 69, near Ste-Marguerite Station, is another popular hostelry, **L'Estérel,** a 135-room establishment with a private golf course, beach, swimming pool, tennis courts, and downhill skiing facilities. Its sports complex and convention facilities make it a busy resort. *Fridolin Simard Blvd., L'Esterel, tel. 819/228–2571 or 800/363–3623. MAP rates start from $103 double with packages from $441 for 6 days and 5 nights.*

The Laurentians

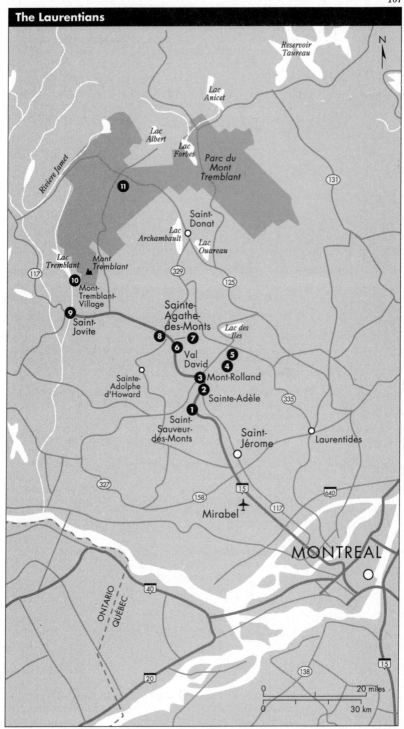

N

Reservoir
Taureau

Lac
Anicet

Lac
Albert

Lac
Forbes

Parc du
Mont
Tremblant

131

Rivière Jamet

11

Saint-
Donat

Lac
Archambault

Lac
Ouareau

329

125

Lac
Tremblant

Mont
Tremblant

117

10

Mont-
Tremblant-
Village

Sainte-
Agathe-
des-Monts

Lac des
Îles

9

Saint-
Jovite

8   7

6

Val
David

5

4

Sainte-
Adolphe
d'Howard

3 Mont-Rolland

2

Sainte-Adèle

335

1

Saint-
Sauveur-
des-Monts

Saint-
Jérôme

Laurentides

327

158   15   640

117

Mirabel

MONTREAL

ONTARIO
QUÉBEC

40

20

138

15

0   20 miles

0   30 km

❻ Children know Val David for its **Santa Claus Village** (tel. 819/
322–2146; admission; open late May–early Oct.). Discriminat-
❼ ing adults come for the **Hôtel la Sapinière,** Canada's first
member of the French association of fine country hotels, the
Relais et Châteaux.

This homey, dark-brown frame hotel with its bright country
flowers provides comfortable accommodations but is best
known for its fine dining room and wine cellar. Under Chef
Marcel Kretz, who makes occasional TV appearances touting a
certain brand of coffee, it has become one of Quebec's, if not
Canada's, better restaurants. In peak season, nonhotel diners
should make reservations a week or two in advance. La
Sapinière is a major convention center, catering to government
summits and high-level meetings.*Val David, Rte. 117, tel. 819/
322–2020 or 800/567–6635. Special week-night rates start from
$99 per person, double occupancy with three complete meals.
Regular double rates range between $228 and $254.*

Val David also has three campgrounds all along Route 117, La
Belle Étoile, Camping Laurentien, and Le Montagnais.

St-Sauveur, Exit 60 off the Autoroute, is the focal point for area
resorts. During the past decade this town has grown so swiftly
that vacationers who once camped on its outskirts say they
barely recognize it.

The surrounding ski hill complexes of Mont-Habitant and
Mont-St-Sauveur offer ever-increasing condo developments,
lodges, hotels, motels, and inns at the foot of, or just a mile or so
from, mountain slopes. Mont-Habitant alone features two 40-
room and six 100-room lodges in addition to 125 motel rooms.
Mont St-Sauveur's slopes are dotted with modern condo units.

Despite all this development, St-Sauveur itself has managed to
add more than 60 good restaurants and a shopping mall without
ruining its character. Its gleaming white-spired church, Eglise
St. Sauveur, still dominates Principal Street Classical concerts
are held here every Tuesday evening during July and August
(tel. 819/227–2663). Up and down this main street, crafts
shops, hand-made jewelry stores, and fashion boutiques are in-
terspersed with the bright awnings and flowers of outdoor café
terrasses, and French restaurants. **Auberge St-Denis** is a classic
Quebec inn that has earned the title of "Relais Gourmand" for
its cuisine. Don't eat and run . . . it is one of the nicer places to
base a Laurentian visit. *62 St. Denis St., tel. 514/227–4766.
Rates range from $120 single to $220 double.*

The **Théâtre de Mont Saint-Sauveur** (22 Rue Claude, tel. 514/
227–4638) features French-language summer comedies and a
boîte à chansons. Outside of St-Sauveur the **Mont Saint-
Sauveur Aquatic Park** and tourist center (exits 58 or 60), keep
the kids happy with slides, wave pools, snack bars, etc.

About 40 miles (64 kilometers) from Montreal, overlooking Lac
❽ des Sables, is **Ste-Agathe-des-Monts,** the largest commercial
center for ski communities farther north. This lively resort
area attracts campers to its spacious "Camping Ste-Agathe"
(Rte. 329, tel. 819/326–5577); bathers to the municipal beach;
and lake cruises on the *Alouette* touring launch.

Farther north lie two of Quebec's best known ski resorts, Gray
Rocks, and Mount Tremblant Lodge, now part of Station
Touristique de Mont Tremblant.

Exiting off the end of the Autoroute, motorists first come to **Gray Rocks,** in St-Jovite. The oldest ski resort in the Laurentians, it was founded by the Wheeler family more than three generations ago. A sprawling wooden hotel with modern chalets and units, it overlooks Lac Ouimet. Gray Rocks has its own private mountain ribboned by 18 ski runs. The winter ski weeks and weekends, including cross-country, are good value for the money, as are the summer tennis packages. Gray Rocks also runs the more intimate Auberge Le Château with 36 rooms farther along on Route 327 North. *Rte. 327N, tel. 819/425–2771 or 800/567–6767. Standard rooms begin at $143, $614 for condominium accommodating more than 2 persons.*

Mount Tremblant Lodge, on nine-mile Lac Tremblant, is the northernmost resort of the Laurentians. As with most other area resorts, winter is the busiest time at Mount Tremblant with skiers tackling the Laurentians's steepest slopes. The partying is livelier too, with lots of après-ski bars in the hotel and immediate area. In summer, guests swim, windsurf and sail. Mount Tremblant Lodge has a 9-hole golf course, and horseback riding and tennis are also available. *Lac Tremblant, tel. 819/425–8711 or 800/567–6761. Regular rates run from $134 single to $890 for condominium accommodations for more than 2 persons.*

Across the lake is **Cuttle's Mount Tremblant Club,** a hotel and condominium complex that uses the mountain for its skiing. Cuttle's was renovated in 1988, and an indoor pool and exercise facility are planned for 1989. *Chemin Lac Tremblant Nord, tel. 819/425–2731. Regular rates vary between $125 single and $292 double.*

The mountain and the hundreds of square miles of wilderness beyond it comprise **Mount Tremblant Park.** Created in 1894, this was once the home of the Algonquin Indians, who called this area *Manitonga Soutana,* meaning "mountain of the spirits." Today it is a vast wildlife sanctuary of more than 500 lakes and rivers protecting some 230 species of birds and animals, including moose, deer, bear, and beaver. In the winter, its trails are used by cross-country skiers, snowshoers, and snowmobile enthusiasts. Moose hunting is allowed in season, and camping and canoeing are the main summer activities. There are three campgrounds with a total of 1,500 sites: Lac Monroe (which also has a park reception center), Lac Chat, and Lac Lajoie. In addition there are approximately 20 cottages for rent. Other park reception centers are in St-Donat and St-Come (tel. 819/688–2281).

Estrie

Estrie (before Bill 101 known as the Eastern Townships) refers to the area in the southeast corner of Quebec Province, bordering Vermont and New York State. Its northern Appalachian hills, rolling down to placid lakeshores, were first home to the Abenaki Indians, long before "summer people" built their cottages and horse paddocks here. The Indians are gone, but the names they gave to the region's recreational lakes remain— Memphremagog, Massawippi, Megantic.

Estrie was left largely unsettled by early French colonists who concentrated on northern Quebec, save for a few trappers.

They were initially populated by United Empire Loyalists fleeing the American War of Independence and, later, the newly
created United States of America, to continue living under the
English king in British North America. They were followed,
around 1820, by the first wave of Irish immigrants, ironically,
Catholics fleeing their country's union with Protestant England. Some 20 years later the Potato Famine sent more Irish
pioneers to the Townships.

Estrie became more Gallic after 1850, as French-Canadians
moved in to work on the railroad and in the lumber industry,
and later to mine asbestos at Thetford. Around the turn of the
century, English families from Montreal and Americans from
the border states discovered the region and began "summer-
ing" at cottages along the lakes.

Today the summer communities fill up with equal parts French
and English visitors, though year-round residents are primarily French. Nevertheless, Townshippers are proud of both their
Loyalist heritage and Quebec roots. They boast of "Loyalist
tours" and Victorian gingerbread homes, and in the next
breath, direct visitors to the snowmobile museum in Valcourt,
where, in 1937, native son Joseph-Armand Bombardier built
the first *moto-neige* in his garage. (Bombardier's inventions
were the basis of one of Canada's biggest industries, supplying
New York City and Mexico City with subway cars and other
rolling stock).

Over the last two decades, Estrie has developed from a series of
quiet farm communities and wood-frame summer homes to a
thriving all-season resort area. In winter, skiers flock to nine
downhill centers and 26 cross-country trails. By early spring,
the sugar shacks are busy with the new maple syrup. Estrie's
southerly location makes this the balmiest corner of Quebec,
notable for its spring skiing. In summer, boating, swimming,
and bike riding take over. And every fall the inns are booked
solid with "leaf peepers" eager to take in the brilliant foliage.

Important Addresses and Numbers

Tourist In Montreal, information about Estrie is available at the **Que-**
Information **bec Tourism Office** (2 Place Ville Marie at University St., tel.
514/873–2015). Regional provincial tourist offices are located in
the towns of Bromont, Granby, Lac-Brome, Magog, Sherbrooke, and Sutton.

For lodging information, contact: Association Touristique de
L'Estrie (2338 King St. W, Sherbrooke PQ J1I 1C6, tel. 819/
566–7404).

Getting Around

By Car Take Autoroute 10 East from Montreal or from New England
on U.S. 91, which becomes Autoroute 55 as it crosses the border at Rock Island.

Exploring

*Numbers in the margin correspond with points of interest on
the Estrie map.*

Estrie (Eastern Townships)

Thetford Mines

FRONTENAC

Arthabaska

Victoriaville

Sherbrooke

216

Drummondville

143

222

1

5

55

CANADA
U. S.

NEW HAMPSHIRE

N

222

3
Mont Orford

Magog

Saint-Benoît-du-Lac

Lac Memphrémagog

91

20

Rivière Saint-François

122

222

4
Valcourt

112

2
Granby

10

Lac Brome
(Knowlton)

VERMONT

Lac Saint-Pierre

112

Chambly

89

20

St. Lawrence River

Lake Champlain

40

MONTREAL

15

20

87

15

20

ONTARIO
QUEBEC

40

15

20

NEW YORK

20 miles

30 km

0

0

1 The region's capital is the city of **Sherbrooke,** named in 1818 for Canadian Governor General Sir John Coape Sherbrooke. It boasts a number of art galleries, the Museum of Fine Arts (1300 Portland Blvd.; admission free; open Sun.–Fri. 1–5 PM), and the historic Domaine Howard, headquarters of the Townships' historic society, which conducts city tours from this site weekdays from June to September.

2 However, **Granby,** about 50 miles (80 kilometers) from Montreal, is where Estrie more or less begins. This town is best known for the **Granby Zoo,** housing some 1,200 animal specimens in a complex including amusement park rides, and souvenir shops as well as play and picnic grounds. *137 Bourget St., tel. 514/ 372–9113. Admission: $7 adults, $3.75 students, $1 children 1–4. Open daily from early May to early October.*

Granby is also gaining repute as the Townships' gastronomic capital. The month-long Festival Gastronomique attracts more than 10,000 *gastronomes* each October, who use the festival's "gastronomic passport" to sample the cuisines at several dining rooms. To reserve a passport, write: *Festival gastronomique de Granby et région, Box 882, Granby PO J2G 8W9, tel. 514/372– 7272.*

The **Yamaska** recreation center on the outskirts of town features sailboarding, swimming, and picnicking all summer and cross-country skiing and snowshoeing in winter.

Granby and its environs is one of Quebec's foremost regions for traditional Quebecois cuisine, here called *la fine cuisine estrienne.* Specialties include mixed game meat pies like *cipaille* and sweet, salty dishes like ham and maple syrup. Actually, maple syrup—on everything and in all its forms—is a mainstay of Quebecois dishes as Estrie is one of Quebec's main sugaring regions.

Every March the combination of sunny days and cold nights causes the sap to run in the maple trees. Sugar shacks or *cabanes à sucre* go into operation boiling the sap collected from the trees in buckets (now, at some places, complicated tubing and vats do the job). The many commercial shacks scattered over the area host "sugaring offs," tours of the operation, the tapped maple trees, boiling vats, etc., and *tire sur la neige,* when hot syrup is poured over cold snow to give it a taffy consistency just right for "pulling" and eating. A number of *cabanes* offer hearty meals of ham, baked beans, and pancakes all drowned in maple syrup. A short list of typical sugar shacks includes **Érablière Robert Lauzier at Ayer's Cliff** on chemin Audet (tel. 819/838–4433); the *cabanes* belonging to the **Bolducs** at Cookshire, on Route 253 (tel. 819/875–3167) and 525 chemin Lower (tel. 819/875–3022). For those who prefer to skip the meal but enjoy the pull, there's **Cabane rustique,** Roxton Pond, 559 3ième Rang (Third Rd.). Call the *cabanes* especially if the season has not been good, to make sure the sugar shacks are operating (tel. 514/372–1522).

In addition to maple sugar, cloves, nutmeg, cinnamon, and pepper—the same spices used by the first settlers—have never gone of out of fashion here, and local restaurants make good use of them in their distinctive dishes. In Sherbrooke, make a reservation for the *Restaurant Au P'tit Sabot (1410 King St. W, tel. 819/563–0262),* which recently won an award for the best local-style eatery in the entire region. Other well-reputed restaurants include *Auberge de l'Étoile* (Magog, tel. 819/843–6521), *Hotel Bromont* (Bromont, tel. 514/534–2378), *and Auberge Hatley* (North Hatley, tel. 819/842–2451).

In the past two decades Estrie has developed into a scenic and increasingly popular ski center, although it is still less crowded and commercialized than the Laurentians.

The larger downhill slopes include **Bromont** (site of the 1986 World Cup) with 26 trails, **Mont Orford** with 33, **Owl's Head** with 21, and **Mont Sutton** with 38. The steepest drop, 2,000 feet (3,700 meters) is at Orford. All four resorts feature interchangeable lift tickets so skiers can test out all the major runs in the area. (Ski East, tel. 819/564–8989).

The area's 26 cross-country trails are peaceful getaways. Trails at Bromont criss-cross the site of the 1976 Olympic equestrian center. The *Skiwippi* network covers some 20 miles (32 kilometers) leading skiers from one country inn to another (including Hatley Inn, Ripplecove Inn, and Hovey Manor).

Valcourt is the birthplace of the inventor of the snowmobile, so it follows that this is a world center for the sport with 1,000-plus miles of paths cutting through the woods and meadows. Every February, Valcourt holds a snowmobile festival with races and demonstrations. Maps outlining scenic routes are available through Estrie tourist associations (tel. 819/566–7404).

Orford and Bromont have highly developed ski resort facilities with condos, hotels, motels, and lodges adding to the rustic inns in nearby villages. Orford alone has eight different complexes from the exclusive **Auberge Estrimont** (44 ave. de l'Auberge, tel. 819/843–1616 or 800/567–3402; up to $285 per night double), **Motel Tremblay** (1215 chemin de la Montagne, tel. 819/847–1979; $45). Condo developments here are often the most convenient accommodations for families. There are many to choose from including: **Village Roussillon** (Magog-Orford, tel. 819/847–2131 or 800/567–3535) and **O'berge du Village** (condo-hotel) (261 rue Merry S, tel. 819/843–6566 or 800/567–6089).

Sutton has a number of moderately priced inns close to its slopes and trails including **Hotel La Paimpolaise** (chemin du Ski, tel. 514/538–3213), **Auberge Le Refuge** (33 Maple, tel. 514/538–3802), and **Auberge Schweizer** (chemin Schweizer, tel. 514/538–2129).

Bromont, Orford, and Sutton are active all summer as well. Bromont and Orford are "stations touristiques" (tourist centers), meaning they offer a wide range of activities in all seasons—boating, camping, golf, horseback riding, swimming, tennis, water parks, cross-country, downhill, snowshoeing, etc.

Orford's regional park is the site of an annual arts festival highlighting classical music, pops as well as chamber orchestra concerts and jazz. Art exhibitions complement the summerlong event. Musicians give concerts in the gracefully designed concert hall or in the park, where they often practice as well, seated among the outdoor sculptures. *Centre d'arts Oxford, Box 280, Magog, Quebec JIX 3W8, tel. 819/843–3981 or in Canada from May to August 800/567–6155.*

As the former Olympic equestrian site, Bromont is horse country and, every mid-July, holds a riding festival (tel. 514/534–3255). A waterslide park—take Exit 78 off Autoroute 10 (tel. 514/534–2200)—and a large flea market (weekends from May to mid-November) are pleasant diversions for those not into horses.

Summer theater is another attraction in Estrie, although the major activity is at French-language repertory companies. Nevertheless, English theater is well served by **The Piggery,** in a former pig barn in **North Hatley** on the shores of Lake Massawippi. An attractive little restaurant serves country suppers prior to the 8 PM curtain during the June through August season (reservations required, tel. 819/842–2606). It was joined in June of 1988 by the Lake Brome Theatre of Knowlton, the old Lakeview Inn transformed into a 200-seat summer stage (tel. 514/243–6183).

With so much to see in this relatively small area, some people like to base themselves at one of the fine old country resorts on Lake Massawippi. **Hovey Manor** is a former private estate dating to 1899 with elegantly furnished rooms, some featuring four-posters and fireplaces. *Box 60, North Hatley, tel. 819/842–2421. 35 rooms. AE, MC, V.*

The **Ripplecove Inn** has an antique feel to it with its old-fashioned rooms, family cottages, and lake views. More modern additions include a winter skating rink and a "wet bar" boat that cruises Massawippi. *700 chemin Ripplecove, Ayer's Cliff, tel. 819/838–4296. 26 rooms. AE, MC, V.*

Both these inns have notable kitchens, but gourmet cuisine is the main attraction at **Hatley Inn.** A member of the Relais & Châteaux, it is home to award-winning chef Guy Bohec. After eating one of his fine meals, guests sleep it off in one of the 21 charmingly decorated rooms in this country manor built in 1903. *Rte. Magog, North Hatley, tel. 819/842–2451.*

French Vocabulary

Words and Phrases

	English	French	Pronunciation
Basics	Yes/no	Oui/non	wee/no
	Please	S'il vous plait	seel voo play
	Thank you (very much)	Merci (beaucoup)	mare-**see** (boh-**koo**)
	You're welcome	De rien	deh ree-**en**
	That's all right	Il n'y a pas de quoi	eel nee ah pah deh kwah
	Excuse me, sorry	Pardon	pahr-**doan**
	Sorry!	Désolé(e)	day-zoh-**lay**
	Good morning/afternoon	Bonjour	bone-**joor**
	Good evening	Bonsoir	Bone-**swar**
	Goodbye	Au revoir	o ruh-**vwar**
	Mr.(Sir)/ Mrs.(Ma'am)/	Monsieur/madame/	meh-see-**ur**/mah-**dahm**
	Miss	mademoiselle	mad-mwah-**zel**
	Pleased to meet you	Enchanté(e)	on-shahn-**tay**
	How are you?	Comment allez-vous?	ko-men-tahl-ay-**voo**
	Very well, thanks	Très bien, merci	tray bee-**en**, mare-**see**
	And you?	Et vous?	ay voo?
Numbers	one	un	un
	two	deux	dew
	three	trois	twa
	four	quatre	**cat**-ruh
	five	cinq	sank
	six	six	seess
	seven	sept	set
	eight	huit	wheat
	nine	neuf	nuf
	ten	dix	deess
	eleven	onze	owns
	twelve	douze	dues
	thirteen	treize	trays
	fourteen	quatorze	ka-torz
	fifteen	quinze	cans
	sixteen	seize	sez
	seventeen	dix-sept	deess-**set**
	eighteen	dix-huit	deess-**wheat**
	nineteen	dix-neuf	deess-**nuf**
	twenty	vingt	vant
	twenty-one	vingt-et-un	vant-ay-**un**
	thirty	trente	trahnt
	forty	quarante	ka-**rahnt**
	fifty	cinquante	sang-**kahnt**
	sixty	soixante	swa-**sahnt**
	seventy	soixante-dix	swa-sahnt-**deess**
	eighty	quatre-vingts	cat-ruh-**vant**

	ninety	quatre-vingt-dix	cat-ruh-vant-**deess**
	one hundred	cent	sahnt
	one thousand	mille	meel

Colors	black	noir	nwar
	blue	bleu	blu
	brown	brun	brun
	green	vert	vair
	orange	orange	o-**ranj**
	pink	rose	rose
	red	rouge	rouge
	violet	violette	vee-o-**let**
	white	blanc	blahnk
	yellow	jaune	jone

Days of the Week	Sunday	dimanche	dee-**mahnsh**
	Monday	lundi	lewn-**dee**
	Tuesday	mardi	mar-**dee**
	Wednesday	mercredi	mare-kruh-**dee**
	Thursday	jeudi	juh-**dee**
	Friday	vendredi	van-dra-**dee**
	Saturday	samedi	sam-**dee**

Months	January	janvier	jan-**vyay**
	February	février	feh-vree-**ay**
	March	mars	mars
	April	avril	a-**vreel**
	May	mai	may
	June	juin	jwan
	July	juillet	jwee-**ay**
	August	août	oot
	September	septembre	sep-**tahm**-bruh
	October	octobre	oak-**toe**-bruh
	November	novembre	no-**vahm**-bruh
	December	décembre	day-**sahm**-bruh

Useful Phrases	Do you speak English?	Parlez-vous anglais?	par-lay vooz ahng-**glay**
	I don't speak French	Je ne parle pas français	jeh nuh parl pah fraun-**say**
	I don't understand	Je ne comprends pas	jeh nuh kohm-prahn **pah**
	I understand	Je comprends	jeh kohm-**prahn**
	I don't know	Je ne sais pas	jeh nuh say **pah**
	I'm American/British	Je suis américain/anglais	jeh sweez a-may-ree-**can**/ ahng-**glay**
	What's your name?	Comment vous appelez-vous?	ko-mahn voo za-pel-ay-**voo**
	My name is . . .	Je m'appelle . . .	jeh muh-**pel** . . .
	What time is it?	Quelle heure est-il?	kel ur et-**il**
	How?	Comment?	ko-**mahn**

When?	Quand?	kahnd
How much is it?	C'est combien?	say comb-bee-**en**
It's expensive/cheap	C'est cher/pas cher	say sher/pa sher
A little/a lot	Un peu/beaucoup	un puh/bo-**koo**
More/less	Plus/moins	ploo/mwa
Enough/too (much)	Assez/trop	a-**say**/tro
I am ill/sick	Je suis malade	jeh swee ma-**lahd**
Please call a doctor	Appelez un docteur	a-pe-lay un dohk-**tore**
Help!	Au secours!	o say-**koor**
Stop!	Arrêtez!	a-ruh-**tay**
Fire!	Au feu!	o fuw
Caution!/Look out!	Attention!	a-tahn-see-**own**

Dining Out

A bottle of . . .	une bouteille de . . .	ewn boo-**tay** deh
A cup of . . .	une tasse de . . .	ewn tass deh
A glass of . . .	un verre de . . .	un vair deh
Ashtray	un cendrier	un sahn-dree-**ay**
Bill/check	l'addition	la-dee-see-**own**
Bread	du pain	due pan
Breakfast	le petit déjeuner	leh pet-**ee** day-zhu-**nay**
Butter	du beurre	due bur
Cheers!	A votre santé!	ah vo-truh sahn-**tay**
Cocktail/aperitif	un apéritif	un ah-pay-ree-**teef**
Dinner	le dîner	leh dee-**nay**
Dish of the day	le plat du jour	leh pla do **zhoor**
Enjoy!	Bon appétit!	bone a-pay-**tee**
Fixed-price menu	le menu	leh may-**new**
Fork	une fourchette	ewn four-**shet**
I am diabetic	Je suis diabétique	jeh swee-dee-ah-**bay-teek**
I am on a diet	Je suis au régime	jeh sweez o ray-**jeem**
I am vegetarian	Je suis végétarien (ne)	jeh swee vay-jay-ta-ree-**en**
I cannot eat . . .	Je ne peux pas manger de . . .	jeh nuh puh pah mahn-**jay** deh
I'd like to order	Je voudrais commander	jeh voo-**dray** ko-mahn-**day**

I'd like . . .	Je voudrais . . .	jeh voo-**dray**
I'm hungry/thirsty	J'ai faim/soif	jay fam/swahf
Is service/the tip included?	Est-ce que le service est compris?	ess keh leh sair-veess ay comb-**pree**
It's good/bad	C'est bon/mauvais	say bon/mo-**vay**
It's hot/cold	C'est chaud/froid	say sho/frwah
Knife	un couteau	un koo-**toe**
Lunch	le déjeuner	leh day-juh-**nay**
Menu	la carte	la cart
Napkin	une serviette	ewn sair-vee-**et**
Pepper	du poivre	due **pwah**-vruh
Plate	une assiette	ewn a-see-**et**
Please give me . . .	Donnez-moi . . .	doe-nay-**mwah**
Salt	du sel	dew sell
Spoon	une cuillère	ewn kwee-**air**
Sugar	du sucre	due **sook**-ruh
Waiter!/Waitress!	Monsieur!/ Mademoiselle!	meh-see-**ur** /mad-mwah-**zel**
Wine list	la carte des vins	la cart day **van**

Menu Guide

French	English
Boisson comprise	Drink included
Garniture au choix	Choice of vegetable accompaniment
Menu à prix fixe	Set menu
Plat du jour	Dish of the day
Selon arrivage	When available
Spécialités locales	Local specialties
Supplément/En sus	Extra charge
Sur commande	Made to order

Breakfast

Confiture	Jam
Croissants	Croissants
Miel	Honey
Oeuf à la coque	Boiled egg
Oeufs au bacon	Bacon and eggs
Oeufs au jambon	Ham and eggs
Oeufs au plat	Fried eggs
Oeufs brouillés	Scrambled eggs
Omelette (nature)	(Plain) omelet
Petits pains	Rolls

Starters

Anchois	Anchovies
Andouille(tte)	Aromatic sausage
Assiette anglaise	Assorted cold cuts
Assiette de charcuterie	Assorted pork products
Bouchée à la reine	Pastry shell filled with creamed sweetbreads and mushrooms
Crépinette	Small, highly seasoned sausage
Crudités	Mixed raw vegetable salad
Escargots	Snails
Hors-d'oeuvre variés	Assorted appetizers
Jambon (de Bayonne)	(Bayonne) ham
Jambonneau	Cured pig's knuckle
Mortadelle	Bologna sausage
Oeufs à la diable	Deviled eggs
Pâté	Liver purée blended with other meat
Quenelles	Light dumplings (fish, fowl, or meat)
Quiche (lorraine)	Tart with a rich, creamy filling of cheese, vegetables, meat, or seafood
Saucisson	Cold sausage
Soufflé	Puffy dish made of egg whites flavored with cheese, vegetables, or seafood
Terrine	Pâté sliced and served from an earthenware pot
Viande séchée	Cured dried beef

Salads

Salade d'endives	Endive salad
Salade niçoise	Riviera combination salad
Salade panachée	Mixed salad
Salade russe	Diced vegetable salad
Salade de thon	Tuna salad
Salade verte	Green salad

Soups

Bisque	Seafood stew (chowder)
Bouillabaisse	Fish and seafood stew
Crême de . . .	Cream of . . .
Pot-au-feu	Stew of meat and vegetables
Potage	Light soup
Condé	*mashed red beans*
julienne	*shredded vegetables*
Parmentier	*potato*
Soupe	Hearty soup
du jour	*Day's soup*
à l'oignon	*French onion soup*
au pistou	*Provençal vegetable soup*
Velouté de . . .	Cream of . . .
Vichyssoise	Cold leek and potato cream soup

Fish and Seafood

Anguille	Eel
Bar	Bass
Bourride	Fish stew from Marseilles
Brandade de morue	Creamed salt cod
Brochet	Pike
Cabillaud	Fresh cod
Calmars	Squid
Carpe	Carp
Coquilles St-Jacques	Scallops in creamy sauce
Crabe	Crab
Crevettes	Shrimp
Cuisses de grenouilles	Frog's legs
Daurade	Sea bream
Ecrevisses	Cray fish
Eperlans	Smelt
Goujons	Gudgeon
Harengs	Herring
Homard	Lobster
Huîtres	Oysters
Langouste	Spiny lobster
Langoustines	Dublin bay prawns, scampi
Lotte	Burbot
Lotte de mer	Angler
Loup	Sea brass
Maquereau	Mackerel
Matelote	Fish stew in wine
Merlan	Whiting
Morue	Cod
Moules	Mussels

Palourdes	Clams
Perche	Perch
Poulpes	Octopus
Raie	Skate
Rascasse	Fish used in bouillabaisse
Rouget	Red mullet
Saumon	Salmon
Scampi	Prawns
Sole	Sole
Thon	Tuna
Truite	Trout

Methods of Preparation

Au four	Baked
Frit	Fried
Grillé	Grilled
Mariné	Marinated
Poché	Poached
Sauté	Sautéed
Fumé	Smoked
Cuit à la vapeur	Steamed

Meat

Agneau	Lamb
Boeuf	Beef
Boeuf bourguignon	Beef stew with vegetables, braised in red Burgundy wine
Boulettes de viande	Meatballs
Brochette	Kabob
Carbonnade flamande	Beef slices and onions braised in beer (Belgian specialty)
Cassoulet toulousain	Casserole of white beans and meat
Cervelle	Brains
Chateaubriand	Double fillet steak
Choucroute garnie	Sauerkraut served with sausages and cured pork
Contre-filet	Loin strip steak
Côte	Rib
Côte de boeuf	T-bone steak
Côtelettes	Chops
Entrecôte	Rib or rib-eye steak
Epaule	Shoulder
Escalope	Cutlet
Filet	Fillet steak
Foie	Liver
Gigot	Leg
Langue	Tongue
Médaillon	Tenderloin steak
Pieds de cochon	Pig's feet
Porc	Pork
Ragoût	Stew
Ris de veau	Veal sweetbreads
Rognons	Kidneys
Saussices	Sausages
Selle	Saddle
Steak/steack	Steak (always beef)
Tournedos	Tenderloin of T-bone steak
Veau	Veal

Bleu	Very rare
Saignant	Rare
A point	Medium
Bien cuit	Well-done
A l'étouffée	Stewed
Au four	Baked
Bouilli	Boiled
Braisé	Braised
Frit	Fried

Methods of Preparation

Grillé	Grilled
Rôti	Roast
Sauté	Sautéed

Game and Poultry

Caille	Quail
Canard à l'orange	Duck braised with oranges and orange liqueur
Canard/caneton	Duck/duckling
Cerf/chevreuil	Venison (red/roe)
Coq au vin	Chicken stewed in red wine
Dinde/dindonneau	Turkey/young turkey
Faisan	Pheasant
Grive	Thrush
Lapin	Rabbit
Lièvre	Wild hare
Oie	Goose
Perdrix/perdreau	Partridge/young partridge
Pigeon/pigeonneau	Pigeon/squab
Pintade/pintadeau	Guinea fowl/young guinea fowl
Poularde	Fattened pullet
Poule au pot	Stewed chicken with vegetables
Poulet	Chicken
Poussin	Spring chicken
Sanglier/marcassin	Wild boar/young wild boar
Suprême de volaille	Chicken breast
Volaille	Fowl

Vegetables

Artichaut	Artichoke
Asperge	Asparagus
Aubergines	Eggplant
Carottes	Carrots
Champignons	Mushrooms
Chicorée	Chicory
Chou (rouge)	(Red) cabbage
Chou-fleur	Cauliflower
Choux de Bruxelles	Brussels sprouts
Courgette	Zucchini
Cresson	Watercress
Endives	Endive
Epinards	Spinach
Fèves	Broad beans
Haricots blancs/verts	White kidney/French beans

Laitue	Lettuce
Lentilles	Lentils
Oignons	Onions
Petits pois	Peas
Poireaux	Leeks
Poivrons	Peppers
Radis	Radishes
Ratatouille	Casserole of stewed eggplant, onions, green peppers and zucchini
Tomates	Tomatoes

Spices and Herbs

Ail	Garlic
Cerfeuil	Chervil
Estragon	Tarragon
Fines herbes	Mixture of herbs
Laurier	Bay leaf
Marjolaine	Majoram
Moutarde	Mustard
Persil	Parsley
Piment	Pimiento
Poivre	Pepper
Romarin	Rosemary

Potatoes, Rice, and Noodles

Nouilles	Noodles
Pâtes	Pasta
Pommes (de terre)	Potatoes
Julienne	*matchsticks*
dauphine	*mashed and deep-fried*
duchesse	*mashed with butter and egg-yolks*
en robe des champs	*in their jackets*
frites	*french fries*
mousseline	*mashed*
nature/vapeur	*boiled/steamed*
Riz	Rice
pilaf	*boiled in bouillon with onions*

Sauces and Preparations

Béarnaise	Vinegar, egg yolks, white wine, shallots, tarragon
Béchamel	White sauce
Bordelaise	Mushrooms, red wine, shallots, beef marrow
Bourguignonne	Red wine, herbs
Chasseur	Wine, mushrooms, onions, shallots
Diable	Hot-pepper
Forestière	Mushrooms
Hollandaise	Egg yolks, butter, vinegar
Indienne	Curry
Madère	With Madeira wine
Marinière	White wine, mussel broth, egg yolks
Meunière	Brown butter, parsley, lemon juice
Périgueux	With goose or duck liver purée and truffles

Poivrade	Pepper sauce
Provençale	Onions, tomatoes, garlic
Tartare	Mayonnaise flavoured with mustard and herbs
Vinaigrette	Vinegar dressing

Cheese

boursin, brie, cantal, cheddar canadien, comté, saint-paulin, tomme de Savoie	*Mild*
bleu de Bresse, camembert, cheddar fort, munster, parmesan, pont-l'évêque, roquefort	*Sharp*
edam, emmenthal, gruyère, vacherin	*Swiss*
feta (Greek), St. marcellin,	*Goat's milk*
Croque-madame	Toasted chicken and cheese sandwich
Croque-monsieur	Toasted ham and cheese sandwich
Ramequin	Small cheese tart
Tarte au fromage	Cheese tart

Fruits and Nuts

Abricot	Apricot
Amandes	Almonds
Ananas	Pineapple
Banane	Banana
Bleuets	Blueberries
Cassis	Blackcurrants
Cerises	Cherries
Citron	Lemon
Cacahouètes	Peanuts
Dattes	Dates
Figues	Figs
Fraises	Strawberries
Framboises	Raspberries
Fruits secs	Dried fruit
Groseilles	Redcurrants
Mandarine	Tangerine
Marrons	Chestnuts
Melon	Melon
Mûres	Blackberries
Nectarine	Nectarine
Noisettes	Hazelnuts
Noix	Walnuts
Noix de coco	Coconut
Orange	Orange
Pamplemousse	Grapefruit
Pastèque melon d'eau	Watermelon
Pêche	Peach
Poire	Pear
Pomme	Apple
Pruneaux	Prunes
Prunes	Plums
Raisin blanc/noir	Green/blue grapes
Raisins secs	Raisins

Dessert

Coupe (glacée)	Sundae
Crème caramel	Caramel pudding
Crème Chantilly	Whipped cream
Crêpe suzette	Thin pancakes simmered in orange juice and flambéd with orange liqueur
Flan Cossetarde	Custard
Gâteau au chocolat	Chocolate cake
Glace Crème glacée	Ice-cream
Mousse au chocolat	Chocolate pudding
Omelette norvégienne	Baked Alaska
Poire Belle Hélène	Pear with vanilla ice-cream and chocolate sauce
Profiterole	Puff pastry filled with whipped cream or custard
Sabayon	Creamy dessert of egg yolks, wine, sugar and flavouring
Sorbet	Water ice
Soufflé au Grand-Marnier	Soufflé made of orange liqueur
Tarte aux pommes	Apple pie
Tartelette	Small tart
Tourte	Layer cake
Vacherin glacé	Ice-cream cake

Alcoholic Drinks

Sec	Straight
Avec des glaçons	On the rocks
A l'eau	With water
Apéritifs	*Cocktails*
Kir/blanc-cassis	Chilled white wine mixed with blackcurrant syrup
Bière	*Beer*
Blonde/brune	Light/dark
Vins	*Wine*
Blanc	White
Brut	Very dry
Corsé	Full-bodied
Doux	Sweet
Léger	Light
Mousseux	Sparkling
Rosé	Rosé
Rouge	Red
Sec	Dry
Autres boissons alcoolisées	*Other alcoholic drinks*
Calvados	Apple brandy
Cognac	Brandy
Kirsch	Cherry brandy
Liqueur	Cordial
Poire Williams	Pear brandy
Porto	Port

Nonalcoholic Drinks

Café	Coffee
noir	*black*
crème	*cream*
au lait	*with milk*
décaféiné	*caffein-free*
espresso	*espresso*
Chocolat (chaud)	(Hot) chocolate
Eau minérale	Mineral water
gazeuse	*carbonated*
non gazeuse	*still*
Ginger ale	Ginger ale
Jus de . . .	. . . juice (see fruit)
Lait	Milk
limonade	Lemonade
Orangeade	Orangeade
Schweppes	Tonic water
Thé	Tea
crème/citron	*with milk/lemon*
glacé	*iced tea*
Tisane	Herb tea

Conversion Tables

Distance

Miles/Kilometers To change miles to kilometers, multiply miles by 1.61.
To change kilometers to miles, multiply kilometers by .621.

Km to Mi	Mi to Km
1 = .62	1 = 1.6
2 = 1.20	2 = 3.2
3 = 1.9	3 = 4.8
4 = 2.5	4 = 6.4
5 = 3.2	5 = 8.1
6 = 3.8	6 = 9.8
7 = 4.4	7 = 11.4
8 = 5.1	8 = 13.0
9 = 5.7	9 = 14.6

Feet/Meters To change feet to meters, multiply feet by .305.
To change meters to feet, multiply meters by 3.28.

Meters to Feet	Feet to Meters
1 = 3.3	1 = .31
2 = 6.6	2 = .61
3 = 9.8	3 = .92
4 = 13.1	4 = 1.2
5 = 16.4	5 = 1.5
6 = 19.7	6 = 1.8
7 = 23.0	7 = 2.1
8 = 26.2	8 = 2.5
9 = 29.5	9 = 2.8

Liquid Volume

U.S. Gallons/Liters To change U.S. gallons to liters, multiply gallons by 3.79.
To change liters to U.S. gallons, multiply liters by .264.

Liters to U.S. Gal.	U.S. Gal. to Liters
1 = .26	1 = 3.8
2 = .53	2 = 7.6
3 = 7.9	3 = 11.4
4 = 1.1	4 = 15.1
5 = 1.3	5 = 18.9
6 = 1.6	6 = 22.7
7 = 1.8	7 = 26.5

Index

Personal Itinerary

Departure *Date*

Time

Transportation

Arrival *Date*   *Time*

Departure *Date*   *Time*

Transportation

Accommodations

Arrival *Date*   *Time*

Departure *Date*   *Time*

Transportation

Accommodations

Arrival *Date*   *Time*

Departure *Date*   *Time*

Transportation

Accommodations

Personal Itinerary

Arrival *Date*   *Time*

Departure *Date*   *Time*

Transportation

Accommodations

Arrival *Date*   *Time*

Departure *Date*   *Time*

Transportation

Accommodations

Arrival *Date*   *Time*

Departure *Date*   *Time*

Transportation

Accommodations

Arrival *Date*   *Time*

Departure *Date*   *Time*

Transportation

Accommodations

Addresses

Name	*Name*
Address	*Address*
Telephone	*Telephone*
Name	*Name*
Address	*Address*
Telephone	*Telephone*
Name	*Name*
Address	*Address*
Telephone	*Telephone*
Name	*Name*
Address	*Address*
Telephone	*Telephone*
Name	*Name*
Address	*Address*
Telephone	*Telephone*
Name	*Name*
Address	*Address*
Telephone	*Telephone*
Name	*Name*
Address	*Address*
Telephone	*Telephone*

Fodor's Travel Guides

U.S. Guides

Alaska
American Cities
The American South
Arizona
Atlantic City & the
New Jersey Shore
Boston
California
Cape Cod
Carolinas & the
Georgia Coast
Chesapeake
Chicago
Colorado
Dallas & Fort Worth
Disney World & the
Orlando Area

The Far West
Florida
Greater Miami,
Fort Lauderdale,
Palm Beach
Hawaii
Hawaii (Great Travel
Values)
Houston & Galveston
I-10: California to
Florida
I-55: Chicago to New
Orleans
I-75: Michigan to
Florida
I-80: San Francisco to
New York

I-95: Maine to Miami
Las Vegas
Los Angeles, Orange
County, Palm Springs
Maui
New England
New Mexico
New Orleans
New Orleans (Pocket
Guide)
New York City
New York City (Pocket
Guide)
New York State
Pacific North Coast
Philadelphia
Puerto Rico (Fun in)

Rockies
San Diego
San Francisco
San Francisco (Pocket
Guide)
Texas
United States of
America
Virgin Islands
(U.S. & British)
Virginia
Waikiki
Washington, DC
Williamsburg,
Jamestown &
Yorktown

Foreign Guides

Acapulco
Amsterdam
Australia, New Zealand
& the South Pacific
Austria
The Bahamas
The Bahamas (Pocket
Guide)
Barbados (Fun in)
Beijing, Guangzhou &
Shanghai
Belgium & Luxembourg
Bermuda
Brazil
Britain (Great Travel
Values)
Canada
Canada (Great Travel
Values)
Canada's Maritime
Provinces
Cancún, Cozumel,
Mérida, The
Yucatán
Caribbean
Caribbean (Great
Travel Values)

Central America
Copenhagen,
Stockholm, Oslo,
Helsinki, Reykjavik
Eastern Europe
Egypt
Europe
Europe (Budget)
Florence & Venice
France
France (Great Travel
Values)
Germany
Germany (Great Travel
Values)
Great Britain
Greece
Holland
Hong Kong & Macau
Hungary
India
Ireland
Israel
Italy
Italy (Great Travel
Values)
Jamaica (Fun in)

Japan
Japan (Great Travel
Values)
Jordan & the Holy Land
Kenya
Korea
Lisbon
Loire Valley
London
London (Pocket Guide)
London (Great Travel
Values)
Madrid
Mexico
Mexico (Great Travel
Values)
Mexico City & Acapulco
Mexico's Baja & Puerto
Vallarta, Mazatlán,
Manzanillo, Copper
Canyon
Montreal
Munich
New Zealand
North Africa
Paris
Paris (Pocket Guide)

People's Republic of
China
Portugal
Province of Quebec
Rio de Janeiro
The Riviera (Fun on)
Rome
St. Martin/St. Maarten
Scandinavia
Scotland
Singapore
South America
South Pacific
Southeast Asia
Soviet Union
Spain
Spain (Great Travel
Values)
Sweden
Switzerland
Sydney
Tokyo
Toronto
Turkey
Vienna
Yugoslavia

Special-Interest Guides

Bed & Breakfast
Guide: North America
1936...On the
Continent

Royalty Watching
Selected Hotels of
Europe

Selected Resorts
and Hotels of the U.S.
Ski Resorts of North
America

Views to Dine by
around the World